Country Store
Candy Cookbook

By
Mildred Brand

Editor: Jill Nickerson
Layout Artist: Janet Kumbier
Production: Sally Manich, Sue Flower
Photographer: Gerald Koser

Candy making equipment and supplies
mentioned in this book can usually be found in
cake decorating or craft stores.
They can also be mail-ordered from:

The Country Kitchen
3225 Wells Street
Fort Wayne IN 46808

Library of Congress Catalog Card Number 84-61390
ISBN: 0-89821-063-1
©1984 Reiman Publications, Inc., Post Office Box 572, Milwaukee WI 53201

Contents

Home Made Candies

NET WT. 16 OZ. (1 LB.)

Introduction

CHOCOLATE

In this book, milk chocolate compound will be referred to as 'sweet' chocolate flavored compound. The ingredients in a recipe will indicate when real chocolate is recommended for best results.

CHOCOLATE THERMOMETERS

A microwave thermometer can be used for testing the chocolate. Be sure the chocolate covers the stem of the thermometer for an accurate reading. Good thermometers specifically made for chocolate and dairy products are available.

TEMPERATURES FOR DIPPING

Real milk chocolate—86°-89°
Real semi-sweet chocolate—89°-91°
Compound coatings—96°-98°

DIPPING WITH REAL CHOCOLATE

While real chocolate can be used in cooking, baking and some candies without dipping, it must be tempered when used for molding or covering of fondant centers, nuts, bars and other candies. Tempering requires practice and patience.

Chocolate comes to you in perfect temper from the manufacturer. The temper is broken when chocolate is melted. Fine crystals in the cocoa butter melt at temperatures over 95°. In order to bring chocolate to temper, melt it to 108°, but never over 120°. In order to form fine crystals in cocoa butter which are necessary to produce chocolate with a sheen and snap, the melted chocolate must gradually be cooled. Wafers, finely chopped chocolate or grated chocolate are then added to the warm chocolate to cool and 'seed' it. Wafers or finely chopped chocolate pieces made from tempered chocolate, help bring the melted chocolate to proper temper.

The temperature for dipping should be 86° to 89°. If the chocolate gets below 86°, warm it slightly over warm, not hot, water. Slowly bring the chocolate up to proper dipping temperature. Stir gently during the cooling period.

Letting the chocolate cool to a 'mushy' state or until nearly set up, insures that it will be in temper, providing it is warmed very cautiously. Be sure the temperature does not get higher than 89°.

Another way to temper chocolate is to melt as above, then pour 3/4 of the chocolate on a marble slab. Hold the remaining chocolate over warm, not hot, water. The warm chocolate should be held between 95° and 96°. Work the chocolate with a paddle on the slab until it is cold and nearly set up. Scoop into the warm chocolate and blend together. Check the temperature. The chocolate must not be over 89°. If it is under 86°, warm the chocolate slightly over warm water.

If the chocolate should get too warm, start over by warming the mixture to 108°, then cooling it down again.

Shown on opposite page: Spearmints, No-Cook Lemon Creams, Cut-Out Mints, Cream Cheese.

TESTING FOR PROPER TEMPER

When you feel chocolate is properly tempered, dip a candy center or dab a thin coating on a cold surface. It should start to set up in a couple of minutes and have a nice sheen when completely set. Keep tepid water under properly tempered chocolate.

A good way to hold chocolate at the proper temperature is to keep the double boiler with tepid water on a warming tray with a thermostatic control set on low. Another pot of melted untempered chocolate, kept at about 96°, is useful as small amounts of this chocolate may be added to tempered chocolate. This will keep it warm and also replenish the chocolate as you dip.

While dipping from tempered chocolate, frequently add a tablespoon of warm untempered chocolate. Stir until combined. It is very important to stir thoroughly as you work with the chocolate.

WHEN STREAKING APPEARS

Most people who have worked with real chocolate have had the experience of finding dipped chocolates looking lovely but in a few hours were disappointingly filled with white streaks. This is the result of chocolate that has not been tempered properly. Dipping centers in chocolate which is too cold as well as dipping in chocolate which has been warmed too much after the cooling process, will cause streaking and a dull finish.

CHOCOLATE AND CHOCOLATE FLAVORED COMPOUNDS

Chocolate and chocolate compounds are being widely used today by novice candy makers as well as professionals. Real chocolate contains cocoa butter made from cocoa beans while compound chocolate contains vegetable fat, substituting coconut oil for cocoa butter in high quality coatings.

Real chocolate is more difficult to use as it must be tempered when used for dipping or molding. It is also more expensive. Compound chocolate and pastel coatings need only to be melted to be used in molds and can be used very successfully for dipping by simply cooling slightly after melting.

MELTING CHOCOLATE OR CHOCOLATE FLAVORED COATING

It is important to avoid getting water or steam into either type of chocolate. Excess heat will also ruin either. Chocolate or compound chocolate may be melted several ways. Block chocolate should be chopped coarsely. In a double boiler bring water to a boil, remove from stove and put the top of the double boiler with chocolate over the hot water. Never boil water under chocolate or chocolate flavored coating or pastel coating. Stir gently until melted.

In a microwave oven, give chocolate or compounds short periods of power, stirring each time. Remove from microwave before chocolate or compound is completely melted and stir. Chocolate or compounds may also be melted in a crock pot or in the oven. In each case, care must be taken that the temperature is set as low as possible. Stir occasionally and give it plenty of time to melt.

DIPPING WITH COMPOUNDS

Always work with chocolate or compound coating in a cool room; 68° is ideal. After the compound is melted, the easiest way to prepare it for dipping is to add a few wafers or small pieces of the same colored coating. Stir gently until the pieces are melted. Test by dipping one center and refrigerate briefly. Coating should not run off and spread.

Chocolate should be thick enough to make a design on the top that will stay. Coating should set up within a few minutes and have a shiny appearance. If the coating dries to a dull finish, it was probably still too warm for dipping. Use two small waxed paper covered trays for dipping. Dip a few, refrigerate, then dip more and change trays. Avoid leaving compound in the refrigerator more than a few minutes as it will pick up moisture.

PAINTING CHOCOLATE MOLDS

Only compound coating comes in colors which can be used to make beautiful pieces of colorful candy. This coating does not need to be tempered or even cooled after it is melted. It may be used for molding and is easy for anyone to enjoy making decorated candy for special occasions.

Melt small amounts of colored coating by placing coating in small glass jars which are placed in very hot water. Or place small amounts of coating in cupcake pan cavities and place the pan on a warming tray. Colored coating may also be placed in custard cups and warmed in a microwave, or fill squeeze bottles with wafers or small pieces of compound coatings, place on a flat pan covered with a kitchen towel and warm in an oven set at the lowest temperature. Give the compound plenty of time to melt. Stir it well. Paint colors desired directly on plastic mold.

Clear plastic molds are easiest to work with as you can check the under side and see how the finished product will look. Small brushes or tiny tips on small squeeze bottles will make applying colored coatings easy. Be sure to apply color thickly enough so that the main color of the mold will not show through.

When colors are applied, chill them very briefly, just long enough to set the coating, then fill the mold with basic color of coating. The basic coating should have been cooled down so it does not melt the colors already applied to the mold. Chill again to set up. Release candy from the mold. When making a solid colored mold, the compound does not need to be cooled down after melting but can be used to fill the mold immediately.

LEFTOVER CHOCOLATE FLAVORED COMPOUND COATINGS AND PASTELS

Any leftover chocolate flavored compound coatings or pastel coatings may be stored and melted to use again. Spread leftover coating thinly on waxed paper and let set up. Chop coarsely and store in a moisture proof plastic bag until you are ready to use it again.

Melt as directed in melting chocolate or chocolate flavored compounds. If the coating has small particles of centers or nuts in, it is better to use it immediately by adding nuts, raisins, rice cereals or one of the several crunchies available and spreading out in a bark.

THE TASTE IS WORTH THE EFFORT

Working with compound chocolate is much easier and the results much more likely to be successful. If comparing the two for taste, you are going to want to master the art of tempering real chocolate. While compound chocolate is satisfactory, real chocolate is superb. Using a thermometer to start working with chocolate will be a help, but eventually the feel of chocolate will be all that is necessary to determine when it is right for dipping.

Equipment

PANS

It is important to use pans large enough to prevent boilovers. Most recipes in this book will suggest a suitable pan size. Heavy pans are necessary for cooking candies with milk and cream while lighter weight pans may be used for candies with sugar, water and corn syrup or cream of tartar. Follow directions for stirring or not stirring carefully. Be sure to cover pans if the recipe indicates this. This eliminates the necessity of washing down crystals from the sides of the pan.

THERMOMETERS

To insure desired result and consistency, a candy thermometer is essential. Various types are available and most work well but all should be tested each day before candy is made. They may tend to vary with changes in atmospheric conditions.

To test, simply immerse the base of thermometer in water and bring the water to boil. Continue boiling until the reading goes no higher. Be sure to read the thermometer at eye level. If the thermometer reads 212°, cook candy as the recipe indicates. If it reads higher or lower, cook candy accordingly.

The most practical kind of candy thermometer has a metal frame including a metal base below the ball of mercury. With this type you can prop the thermometer against the side of the pan, let it rest on the bottom and stir without affecting the temperature reading.

MARBLE SLAB

Many recipes suggest using a marble slab because marble will cool candy faster than other surfaces. Fast cooling also affects the size of crystals formed as candy cools, therefore improves the quality of candy. Granite, while looking like marble, will not cool as fast. Formica may be used but the cooling process will be slower. A piece of marble approximately 24- x 18- x 1-inch can be handled fairly easily and can be stored on edge in a closet. While a marble slab is very helpful in making fondants, fudges and hard candy suckers, it is not essential.

SQUEEZE BOTTLES

Squeeze bottles have proved an invaluable aid in the use of chocolate and chocolate compounds. The larger bottles are used to fill bite size molds quickly and neatly and also for filling or lining larger molds. The smaller size paired with a coupler and a cake decorating tube is used to apply various colors of coatings to the mold before filling it with the basic coating color. Both sizes clean very easily. Simply pour out all coating that will come easily, lay the squeeze bottle on its side in the freezer for 10 minutes. Remove from the freezer and squeeze the bottle to break up the chocolate. Shake out and save to be melted and used again.

It is best to remove the lid and wash it before putting the bottle in the freezer as it will be hard to remove after the bottle is chilled. There is almost no waste.

If working with a number of molds and the coating needs to stay workable, turn the oven on the very lowest setting possible. Place a towel on a pan and lay the bottles with the chocolate on the towel. The low heat of the oven will keep the chocolate coating from setting up and will be ready for use when needed.

Glossary

Chocolate Flavored Coating: Sweet and semi-sweet made with vegetable shortening instead of cocoa butter.

Coconut Dough: A chewy, coconut filling for candy bars and centers.

Coconut Oil: One of the ingredients in man-made chocolate. Used to thin chocolate or soften finished candy and make it less brittle.

Concentrated Flavors: These are available in small bottles with dropper tops. Only a few drops are needed. Excellent for flavoring coatings and fondants.

Dessicated Coconut: Macaroon coconut, a finely cut, dry unsweetened coconut.

Dry Fondant: A commercial powdered cane sugar product used in many easy candy recipes.

Dry Egg Whites: Used where fresh egg white has too much liquid for the candy. Can be used in cakes and icings. To reconstitute, use 8 ounces dry egg white and 1 pint of water mixed together. Gradually add 2-1/2 pints more water. 2 tablespoons of reconstituted egg equals 1 egg white.

Filbert Paste: A smooth filbert (hazel nut) butter used in gourmet candies and pastries.

Food Coloring: Use the concentrated paste or powdered color to avoid changing the consistency of candy.

Glucose: Concentrated corn syrup.

Glycerine: Use food quality glycerine available at cake and candy supply stores or drug stores.

Invertase: A yeast derivative used in fondant centers to make them soft and creamy. Always optional.

Invert Sugar: Cane sugar in liquid form. Improves the quality and keeping properties of candy. May also be purchased.

Lecithin: An emulsifier, made from soybeans, available in health food stores. Keeps the fat from separating from the other ingredients, especially useful in caramel and toffees.

Milk Chocolate: A combination of chocolate liquor, added cocoa butter, sugar and milk or cream. It must contain at least 10% chocolate liquor. It may also contain optional ingredients.

Oils: Very potent. Available in bottles with dropper tops for exact measuring. Excellent for flavoring coatings and candies.

Paramount Crystals: Coconut oil in flake form.

Pastel Coating: White, pink, green, yellow, blue, lavender, red, dark green, orange, butterscotch and peanut butter available.

Raw Chip Coconut: Unsweetened raw coconut in wide flake form used for brittles.

Semi-Sweet Chocolate: A combination of chocolate liquor, added cocoa butter and sugar. It must contain at least 35% chocolate liquor. Most commonly known in the form of semi-sweet chocolate chips.

Sweet Dark Chocolate: A combination of chocolate liquor, added cocoa butter and sugar. It must contain at least 15% chocolate liquor and has a higher proportion of sugar than semi-sweet chocolate.

Breathtaking Mints

Orange Party Candies

1-1/2 cups confectioners' sugar
1/3 cup butter
1/2 cup corn syrup
1/8 teaspoon salt
1-3/4 cups dry fondant
1/8 teaspoon orange oil
Orange food color

In a heavy 2-quart saucepan combine confectioners' sugar, butter, corn syrup and salt. Stir to combine ingredients, bring to full, rolling boil. Remove from heat. Add dry fondant and orange oil; mix well. Pour one-third of mixture on buttered surface to cool. Color other two-thirds with orange food color. Cool on buttered surface. Knead when cool. Cut out larger shapes with orange mint and smaller shapes with white mint. Dampen bottoms of white shapes and place over orange shapes. Press slightly to adhere. **NOTE:** You may also form a long roll with white mint. Roll out orange candy same length and wide enough to wrap around it. Dampen orange rolled out candy very lightly. Place white roll in center of orange candy. Wrap orange candy lightly around white roll; trim any excess. Slice candy.

Butter Mints

2-1/4 cups sugar
1 cup water
4 tablespoons butter
1/4 teaspoon salt
1 teaspoon white vinegar
5 drops peppermint oil
Food coloring, optional

In 2-quart saucepan, combine ingredients. Place over high heat, cover tightly. Cook until steam comes from under lid. Remove lid; insert thermometer. Cook to 260° without stirring. Lower heat slightly as mixture thickens. Pour on buttered surface. If using marble slab, warm slightly before pouring syrup. Let candy cool until comfortably warm. Scoop edges into center of candy. Pull candy. Moisten hands on wet sponge as they become sticky. Pull until candy becomes creamy white and ridges form; about 10 to 15 minutes. Pull candy in long ropes. Twist and cut off pieces with scissors. Drop pieces on buttered surface. As candy cools, move pieces to eliminate

sticking to surface. In several hours or overnight candy will cream and become firm, losing caramel texture. Store in tightly covered container.

Spearmint Creams

1 tablespoon butter
4 tablespoons hot water
1/2 cup non-fat dry milk
1 tablespoon corn syrup
Pinch salt
4 drops spearmint oil
Pink food coloring
3 cups dry fondant

Melt butter in hot water. Add dry milk a little at a time. Mix with wire whisk until smooth. Add corn syrup, salt, flavoring oil and food color. Mix together. Add dry fondant a little at a time. Mixture should be consistency of pie dough. Form into a ball. Let rest on waxed paper until all dry fondant is absorbed into candy and no grains can be seen. Sprinkle hands with confectioners' sugar, roll into small balls. Dip fork into confectioners' sugar and flatten each ball. Let patties dry and form crust on each side. Store in air tight container.

No-Cook Lemon Creams

1 pound confectioners' sugar
1/3 cup butter, softened
Pinch salt
5 drops lemon oil
Yellow food color
1/3 cup corn syrup

Mix 1/2 pound sugar with the rest of ingredients; beat until smooth. Gradually add remainder of sugar, mixing well after each addition. Remove from bowl and knead. Add enough sugar to get pie dough consistency. Can be divided with different flavors and colors. Press into soft rubber mold, turn out immediately.

VARIATIONS:
Lemon Patty Mints: Form mints into balls, roll in sugar and flatten slightly with fork.

Chocolate Covered Mints: Form mints into patties. Allow to dry and dip in melted chocolate.

Cream Cheese Mints

1 3-ounce package cream cheese,
  room temperature
Flavoring, optional
Food coloring, optional
2-1/2 cups confectioners' sugar
Granulated sugar

Beat cream cheese until soft. Add flavoring and coloring. Gradually add confectioners' sugar. Beat smooth after each addition. Knead dough until smooth. If needed, add more sugar to get a pie dough consistency. Form into a small ball. Roll in granulated sugar and press into soft rubber molds. Unmold onto wax paper. Mixture may be formed into balls, rolled in sugar and pressed into patties with a fork.

Pulled Mints

2 cups granulated sugar
1/2 cup water
1/4 cup corn syrup
Food coloring, optional
5 drops peppermint oil
Confectioners' sugar

In a 2-quart saucepan combine sugar, water and corn syrup; cover. Cook until steam comes from under lid. Remove lid, insert thermometer. Add coloring when mixture reaches 250°. Cook candy to 260°. Pour on greased marble slab or other cold surface. Let cool until comfortably warm. Drop peppermint oil over surface. Pull candy until opaque and forms ridges, 8 to 10 minutes. Pull into ropes. Twist and cut into small pieces, dropping in bowl of confectioners' sugar. Sprinkle sugar over top and let mints set overnight. Store in covered jar.

Potato Fondant Mints

1 medium potato, baked
Pinch salt
1 tablespoon butter, softened
5 drops peppermint oil
Food coloring
2 to 4 cups confectioners' sugar

Scoop potato from skin and mash thoroughly. Add ingredients except confectioners' sugar; mix well. Add sugar, 1/2 cup at a time, beating well after each addition. When mixture is heavy, turn out on confectioners' sugar and knead smooth. Add enough confectioners' sugar to form a pie dough like consistency. Chill, knead again. Form into balls and flatten. Let dry enough to form crust. Store in airtight container.

Layered Mints

3 pounds semi-sweet chocolate coating
3 tablespoons paramount crystals
  OR 2 tablespoons corn oil
1/2 pound green coating
1 tablespoon paramount crystals
  OR 1 tablespoon corn oil
1/2 teaspoon peppermint oil

In a double boiler melt semi-sweet coating and 3 tablespoons paramount crystals or oil. Melt green coating and 1 tablespoon paramount crystals in another double boiler. Add peppermint oil to semi-sweet coating. Pour half of semi-sweet coating into an 18- x 12- x 1-inch pan lined with waxed paper; let set up. Keep remaining semi-sweet coating over warm water. Pour green coating over semi-sweet coating. Partially set up. Pour remainder of semi-sweet coating over green layer. Let set up at room temperature. When layers are firm, cut into squares. Do not allow candy to get cold before cutting.

Chocolate Mint Squares

2-1/4 cups dry fondant
1-1/2 tablespoons corn syrup
1/2 cup Milnot
1/4 teaspoon invertase, optional
8 drops peppermint oil
1-1/4 cups sweet chocolate coating
1 cup semi-sweet chocolate coating

In mixing bowl combine dry fondant, corn syrup, Milnot, invertase and peppermint oil. Beat until smooth, about 5 minutes. Melt chocolate coatings together; add to dry fondant mixture. Stop beater, scrape down bowl, beat again. Mixture should be very smooth. Pour into an 8-inch square pan; let set up. Cut into small squares; dip in semi-sweet chocolate coating.

Filbert Truffles

1-1/2 cups real milk chocolate
1/2 cup semi-sweet chocolate
1/2 cup filbert paste
1/3 cup whipping cream
2 tablespoons butter
Cocoa, optional
Chopped nuts, optional

Melt chocolate together. Add filbert paste; blend into chocolate. Scald cream; cool to just warm. Add butter and cream all at once into chocolate mixture. Whip until blended. Chill in freezer or refrigerator until almost firm. Whip until light. Chill again; whip. Wrap in plastic wrap. Refrigerate until firm. Form into balls. Drop in cocoa or finely chopped nuts. Roll in nuts until truffle is completely covered. Place into candy cups.

Chocolate Creams

3-3/4 cups sugar
1-1/2 cups half and half cream
2 tablespoons corn syrup
1/4 teaspoon salt
2 tablespoons butter
1-1/2 cups semi-sweet chocolate

In a 3-quart saucepan combine all ingredients. Cook on medium-low heat until chocolate melts. Stir frequently. Increase heat to medium-high. Gradually lower heat as mixture thickens. Stir occasionally. Cook to 237°. Remove from heat and pour on marble slab or other cold surface. Let cool to comfortably warm. Work with spatula until mixture creams and holds shape. Let set for 5 minutes. Knead and form into balls. Wrap securely, keep in cold place and form into balls when ready to dip in chocolate.

White Truffles

1/2 cup whipping cream
2 cups chopped real white chocolate
3 tablespoons finely chopped cocoa butter
Pinch salt
1/2 teaspoon vanilla
Chocolate for dipping

Scald whipping cream; add chocolate and cocoa butter. Whip with wire whisk. Add salt and vanilla. Chill until nearly solid. Whip with mixer until light and nearly doubled in bulk. Form into balls or pipe out in small mounds using pastry bag. Dip in chocolate.

Pecan Truffles

3-1/2 cups real milk chocolate
1/2 cup whipping cream
3/4 cup finely chopped pecans
Dipping chocolate

Melt real chocolate over hot water or in microwave. Remove from heat before completely melted. Stir to melt. Scald cream; cool to about 130°. Add cream, all at once, to melted chocolate. Beat until smooth. Chill in refrigerator or freezer until mixture is almost solid. It will be a plastic-like consistency. Whip until fluffy and light in color. Fold in pecans. Form into balls and dip. If too soft to dip, cover and refrigerate until mixture can be handled.

Mocha-Honey Truffles

2 cups semi-sweet chocolate
1/4 cup honey
1 teaspoon coffee crystals
2 teaspoons hot water
3 tablespoons butter, softened

Melt chocolate. Heat honey. Dissolve coffee crystals in hot water. Add to honey. Add honey mixture to chocolate. Whip with whisk. Add butter as mixture is beating; refrigerate. When very cold and nearly set up, whip until light and fluffy. Roll into balls. Coat as desired. If dipping in chocolate, let truffles set several hours before dipping. Turn over once to form a crust.

Shown on opposite page: Pecan Truffles, Filbert Truffles, Assorted Truffles.

Maple Nut Centers

1/4 cup butter
2/3 cup brown sugar
4 tablespoons whipping cream
2 cups dry fondant
1/8 teaspoon salt
1/2 cup marshmallow cream
4 drops invertase, optional
1/4 to 1/2 teaspoon maple flavoring
2/3 cup chopped walnuts or pecans

In a heavy 2-quart saucepan melt butter. Add brown sugar. Stir until mixture is bubbling. Add whipping cream. Bring to full, rolling boil. Boil 1-1/2 minutes. Remove from heat. Blend in 1 cup dry fondant and salt. Stir in second cup dry fondant. Mixture will be thick. Blend in marshmallow cream, invertase, flavoring and nuts. Mix together thoroughly. Scrape out of pan and mound on buttered surface to cool. When cool, roll into balls. Dip in chocolate or wrap in plastic film. Store in refrigerator until ready to use.

Cherry Creams

1-1/2 cups granulated sugar
1/4 cup butter
1/4 cup milk
1/4 cup whipping cream
Pinch salt
1/2 cup white coating wafers
3/4 cup pink coating wafers
1-1/4 cups miniature marshmallows
1/2 teaspoon vanilla
5 drops concentrated cherry flavoring
8 maraschino cherries, finely chopped

In a 2-quart saucepan mix sugar, butter, milk, whipping cream and salt. Bring to boil and cook to 238°. Stir occasionally. Remove from heat. Immediately blend in the rest of ingredients. Pour on buttered surface. Let cool and set up. When firm enough to handle, knead *VERY LIGHTLY*. Form into balls. Dip in chocolate. **NOTE:** Excess kneading will cause candy to separate.

Shown on opposite page: Coconut Bon-Bons, Chocolate Fudge Centers, Almond Butter Logs, Maple Nut Centers, Chocolate Buttermints, Raspberry Jellies, Assorted Dipped Candies, Lime Creams, Cherry Creams.

Lime Creams

2-1/2 cups dry fondant, divided
2 teaspoons fresh lime juice
1 teaspoon grated lime rind
1 tablespoon water
1 cup green coating, melted
Dipping chocolate

In a mixing bowl beat dry fondant, lime juice, grated rind and water. Beat until smooth. Add melted coating. Work in 1/2 cup dry fondant. Let set until firm enough to handle. Then form into balls and dip.

Orange Creams

2-3/4 cups granulated sugar
1/2 cup orange juice
1/2 cup half and half cream
5 tablespoons butter
1 teaspoon grated orange rind
Chocolate for dipping

In a 3-quart saucepan mix all ingredients except chocolate. Cook on high heat. Lower heat as mixture reaches 240°. Stir occasionally with thermometer. Pour on marble slab or other cold surface. Let cool slightly. Work while mixture is quite warm. Work with spatula until mixture is creamy and holds shape. Knead smooth. Form into balls and dip. May be well wrapped and refrigerated until ready to use. Let come to room temperature. Form into balls and dip in chocolate.

Orange Centers

4 cups dry fondant, divided
3 tablespoons fresh orange juice
1 tablespoon grated orange rind
1 teaspoon citric acid solution
2 tablespoons butter
Orange food coloring
Dipping chocolate

In a mixing bowl combing 2 cups fondant, orange juice, orange rind and citric acid. Whip until smooth. Add butter, food coloring and remaining fondant. Beat smooth. After 30 minutes, mixture can be rolled into balls and dipped in chocolate.

Easy Chocolate Buttercream Centers

2 cups dry fondant
2 tablespoons invert sugar*
1/4 teaspoon invertase
1/8 teaspoon salt
1/4 teaspoon vanilla
2 tablespoons water
1 cup semi-sweet chocolate wafers, melted
2 tablespoons butter, softened

*Recipe for invert sugar is on page 52. Whip together dry fondant, invert sugar, invertase, salt, vanilla and water. Melt semi-sweet chocolate. Add to beating mixture. Continue beating until light and fluffy. Add butter; beat. Let candy rest 30 minutes or until firm enough to handle. Form into balls; dip in chocolate.

Cherry Centers

3-1/2 cups dry fondant, divided
1/8 teaspoon salt
1 tablespoon dry egg whites
4 tablespoons cherry preserves
8 drops concentrated cherry flavoring
2 tablespoons water
Pink food coloring
Sweet or semi-sweet chocolate, melted

In a large mixing bowl place 2 cups fondant, salt, dry egg whites, cherry preserves, flavoring, water and coloring. Whip until light. Add remainder of dry fondant on slow speed. More or less fondant may be used to get desired consistency. Turn out on waxed paper. Let rest at least 30 minutes. When firm enough to handle, form into balls. Dip in chocolate.

Deluxe Centers

1 cup sweetened condensed milk
1 cup butter
1 teaspoon vanilla
1/8 teaspoon salt
2-1/4 cups dry fondant
4 cups dessicated coconut
4 cups chopped pecans or walnuts
Dipping chocolate

Cream milk, butter, vanilla and salt. Add fondant and coconut. Blend in nuts. chill 1 hour. Form into balls and dip in chocolate. Store in refrigerator.

Lemon Creams

4 cups dry fondant, divided
2 tablespoons fresh lemon juice
1 teaspoon grated lemon rind
1 tablespoon water
2 tablespoons butter
Yellow food coloring
1/2 cup marshmallow cream

In a mixing bowl beat 2 cups dry fondant, juice, lemon rind and water. Add butter and food coloring; beat. Add marshmallow cream. Stir in remaining fondant. Blend together. Let rest 30 minutes. Roll into balls. Dip in chocolate.

Easy Butterscotch Centers

2 cups dry fondant
1/8 teaspoon salt
1/4 teaspoon vanilla
6 drops concentrated butterscotch flavoring
3 tablespoons water
1 cup butterscotch wafers, melted
2 tablespoons butter, softened

In a mixing bowl combine fondant, salt, vanilla, butterscotch flavoring and water. Whip until smooth. Add melted butterscotch wafers. Beat until light and fluffy. Add butter; beat. Mixture will seem soft. Let set 30 minutes. If still too soft to form centers, work in another 1/4 cup dry fondant. Add more water with fondant.

Fondant

2 cups granulated sugar
Pinch salt
1/2 teaspoon cream of tartar
3/4 cup water
1/2 teaspoon vanilla
Sweet OR semi-sweet chocolate, melted

In a 1-quart saucepan cook all ingredients except vanilla and chocolate until steam comes from under the lid. Remove lid, insert thermometer. Cook to 240°. Pour at once on marble slab or other cold surface. Cool to comfortably warm. Work with candy scraper until candy sets up and turns pure white. Add vanilla as candy sets up. If candy should suddenly become hard, break off small pieces; work each in hands until soft and pliable. Work batch in hands, a little at a time. Fondant will remain soft and workable. Dip in melted chocolate.

Rum Nut Balls

1-1/2 cups granulated sugar
4 tablespoons whipping cream
2-2/3 tablespoons whole milk
2 teaspoons butter
2/3 teaspoon corn syrup
Dash salt
16 drops butter rum concentrated flavoring
Chopped nuts
Sweet OR semi-sweet chocolate

In a 2-quart saucepan combine sugar, whipping cream, milk, butter, corn syrup and salt. Cook over high heat. Stir until sugar is moistened; bring to boil. Gradually lower heat as mixture thickens. Cool to 238° without stirring. Pour on a marble slab or other cold surface. Cool to comfortably warm. Work with candy scraper until candy creams. Let rest for 30 minutes. Add flavoring and nuts. Form into balls and dip into chocolate.

Maple-Nut Fondant

3-1/2 cups brown sugar
1/8 teaspoon salt
1/4 cup butter
1/2 cup whipping cream
1/2 cup half and half cream
1/2 teaspoon maple flavoring
1 cup chopped walnuts
Sweet OR semi-sweet chocolate, melted

In a 3-quart saucepan combine sugar, salt, butter, whipping cream and cream. Cook over medium-high heat to 238°. Reduce heat as mixture thickens. Pour on marble slab or other cold surface. Let cool to comfortably warm. Work with fondant paddle until creamy and mixture holds shape. Add flavoring as you work. Knead smooth. Blend in nuts. Form into balls; dip in chocolate.

Easy Cream Fondant

6 tablespoons butter
1 to 2 tablespoons whipping cream
1 pound dry fondant
Food coloring, optional
Flavoring, optional

Scald butter and cream. Let cool. Blend into dry fondant. Knead candy until well blended. Color and flavor as desired.

Coconut Cream Centers

6 tablespoons butter
1 to 2 tablespoons whipping cream
1 pound dry fondant
1 pound coconut dough
Sweet OR semi-sweet chocolate, melted

Scald butter and cream. Let cool. Blend into dry fondant. Knead in coconut dough. Dip into melted chocolate.

Peppermint Patties

2 cups granulated sugar
Pinch salt
1/2 teaspoon cream of tartar
3/4 cup water
1/2 teaspoon vanilla
4 drops peppermint oil
Green food coloring
Semi-sweet chocolate

In a 1-quart saucepan cook sugar, salt, cream of tartar and water until steam comes from under lid. Remove lid; insert thermometer. Cook to 240°. Pour at once on marble slab or other cold surface. Cool to comfortably warm. Work with candy scraper until candy sets up and turns pure white. Add vanilla, peppermint oil and food coloring. Work together with fingertips. Form into small patties 1 inch in diameter and 1/8-inch thick. Let dry until a light crust forms. Dip in melted chocolate.

Vanilla Cream Centers

3 cups granulated sugar
1/8 teaspoon salt
3/4 cup whipping cream
1/2 teaspoon cream of tartar
1/2 teaspoon vanilla
Maple flavoring, optional
Chopped nuts, optional

Combine sugar, salt, whipping cream and cream of tartar. Place over high heat. Stir until sugar is moistened and mixture hot. Continue cooking without stirring. Gradually lower heat as candy thickens. Cook to 240°. Immediately pour candy on cold surface. Let cool to comfortably warm. Work with scraper until candy is smooth, sets up and is off-white in color. Mixture will be very creamy. Add maple flavoring and finely chopped nuts.

Butter Centers

3-1/2 cups sugar
1 cup water
2 tablespoons corn syrup
1/8 teaspoon salt
1 teaspoon vanilla
1/2 cup butter, softened
Dipping chocolate

In a 2-quart saucepan cook sugar, water, corn syrup and salt over high heat until steam comes from under lid. Remove lid, insert thermometer. Cook to 240°, without stirring. Pour on marble slab or cold surface. Cool to comfortably warm. Work with fondant paddle. Add vanilla. When candy loses gloss and begins to get creamy, work in butter. Shape into balls. When candy is completely cool, dip in chocolate or wrap in plastic film. Store in refrigerator until ready to use.

Chocolate Buttercream Delights

2 cups dry fondant
1/8 teaspoon salt
1/4 teaspoon vanilla
3 tablespoons water
1 cup semi-sweet chocolate flavored wafers
2 tablespoons butter, softened
Dipping chocolate

Whip fondant, salt, vanilla and water. Add melted chocolate. Whip until light and fluffy. Add butter; beat. Let rest until firm enough to form into balls. Dip in chocolate.

Peanut Butter Creams

2 cups granulated sugar
Pinch salt
1/2 teaspoon cream of tartar
3/4 cup water
1/2 teaspoon vanilla
Peanut butter
Sweet OR semi-sweet chocolate, melted

In a 1-quart saucepan cook sugar, salt, cream of tartar and water until steam comes from under lid. Remove lid; insert thermometer. Cook to 240°. Pour at once on marble slab or other cold surface. Cool to comfortably warm. Work with candy scraper until candy sets up and turns pure white. Add vanilla and enough peanut butter to

equal half the amount of fondant. Work together with fingertips. Roll into balls. Dip in chocolate.

All Purpose Fondant

4 cups granulated sugar
3/4 cup whipping cream
1/2 cup whole milk
3 tablespoons butter
1 tablespoon corn syrup
1/2 teaspoon salt
Flavoring
Food coloring
Chopped nuts
Sweet OR semi-sweet chocolate, melted

In a 4-quart saucepan, combine sugar, cream, milk, butter, corn syrup and salt. Cook over high heat. Stir until sugar is moistened. Bring to boil. Gradually lower heat as mixture thickens. Cook to 238° without stirring. Pour on a marble slab or other cold surface. Cool to comfortably warm. Work with candy scraper until candy creams. Let rest for 30 minutes. Flavor and color as desired. Makes about 105 pieces.

Stuffed Dates

2 cups granulated sugar
Pinch salt
1/2 teaspoon cream of tartar
3/4 cup water
1/2 teaspoon vanilla
Pitted dates
Granulated sugar

In a 1-quart saucepan cook sugar, salt, cream of tartar and water until steam comes from under lid. Remove lid; insert thermometer. Cook to 240°. Pour at once on marble slab or other cold surface. Cool to comfortably warm. Work with candy scraper until candy sets up and turns pure white. Add vanilla as candy sets up. If candy should suddenly become hard, break off small pieces; work each in hands until soft and pliable. Work batch in hands, a little at a time. Fondant will remain soft and workable. Roll into small oblong pieces. Insert each into pitted date. Roll stuffed dates in fine granulated sugar.

Shown on opposite page: Coconut Bon Bons, Lemon Creams, Assorted Fondants.

Tangy Orange Centers

1-1/2 cups granulated sugar
4 tablespoons whipping cream
2-2/3 tablespoons whole milk
2 teaspoons butter
2/3 teaspoon corn syrup
Dash salt
16 drops orange oil
4 drops concentrated orange food coloring
1 teaspoon citric acid
2 teaspoons water
Sweet OR semi-sweet chocolate, melted

In a 2-quart saucepan combine sugar, whipping cream, milk, butter, corn syrup and salt. Cook over high heat. Stir until sugar is moistened. Bring to a boil. Gradually lower heat as mixture thickens. Cool to 238° without stirring. Pour on a marble slab or other cold surface. Cool to comfortably warm. Work with candy scraper until candy creams. Let rest for 30 minutes. Add oil and coloring. Dissolve citric acid in water. With fingertips, work in 1/8 teaspoon of solution. Form into balls and dip in chocolate.

Buttercreams

2-1/4 cups dry fondant
1 fresh egg white
1/8 teaspoon salt
1/2 teaspoon vanilla
2 tablespoons water
1 cup white coating, melted
3 tablespoons butter
1-1/2 cups dry fondant
Dipping chocolate

In a large mixing bowl combine dry fondant, egg white, salt, vanilla and water. Whip until light. Blend in melted white coating. Stir in butter. Add remainder of dry fondant. Let stand until firm enough to handle. Roll into balls; dip in chocolate.

Peanut Butter Centers

1/2 cup butter
1-1/2 cups peanut butter
1/4 cup corn syrup
3/4 to 1 pound confectioners' sugar
Semi-sweet chocolate, melted

Combine ingredients. Roll into balls and dip in melted chocolate.

Tangy Fruit Creams

6 tablespoons butter
1 to 2 tablespoons whipping cream
1/2 teaspoon citric acid crystals
1 pound dry fondant
Red OR orange food coloring
Sweet OR semi-sweet chocolate, melted

Scald butter and cream. Let cool. Dissolve citric acid crystals in butter and cream mixture. Add dry fondant. Work in food coloring and flavoring. Dip into chocolate.

Chocolate Creams

1-1/2 cups granulated sugar
4 tablespoons whipping cream
2-2/3 tablespoons whole milk
2 teaspoons butter
2/3 teaspoon corn syrup
Dash salt
6 tablespoons semi-sweet chocolate, melted
Sweet OR semi-sweet chocolate, melted

In a 2-quart saucepan combine sugar, whipping cream, milk, butter, corn syrup and salt. Cook over high heat. Stir until sugar is moistened; bring to a boil. Gradually lower heat as mixture thickens. Cool to 238° without stirring. Pour on a marble slab or other cold surface. Cool to comfortably warm. Work with candy scraper until candy creams. Let rest for 30 minutes. Add 3 tablespoons melted chocolate. Form into balls and dip in chocolate.

Caramel Creams

6 tablespoons butter
1 to 2 tablespoons whipping cream
1 pound dry fondant
1 pound caramel
Sweet OR semi-sweet chocolate, melted

Scald butter and cream. Let cool. Blend into dry fondant. Knead in caramel. Dip into chocolate.

Shown on opposite page: Peanut Butter Fudge, Party Fudge, Cherry Fudge, Low Cholesterol Fudge.

Melt-in-Your-Mouth Fudge

Banana-Nut Chocolate Fudge

2 bananas, mashed
1-1/2 cups semi-sweet chocolate wafers
1 cup light brown sugar
2 cups granulated sugar
1/2 cup whole milk
1/2 cup whipping cream
2 tablespoons light corn syrup
1/4 teaspoon salt
4 tablespoons butter
1 teaspoon vanilla
1-1/2 cups chopped walnuts

In heavy 3-quart saucepan combine bananas, chocolate, brown sugar, granulated sugar, milk, cream, corn syrup and salt. Cook on medium-low heat. Stir occasionally until chocolate melts and sugar dissolves. Continue cooking on medium heat, stirring to keep mixture from scorching. Gradually lower heat as mixture thickens; cook to 236°. Immediately pour in mixing bowl. Add butter without stirring. Cool to 115°. Add vanilla. Beat at lowest speed until candy loses gloss. Remove beater from bowl, blend in nuts. Continue mixing by hand until candy begins to hold shape. Quickly spread in an 8-inch square pan. Cut into squares while slightly warm.

Old Fashioned Sugar Fudge

3 cups granulated sugar
1/2 cup cocoa
1/4 teaspoon salt
3/4 cup milk
2 tablespoons butter
1 teaspoon vanilla
1 cup black walnuts

Combine sugar, cocoa and salt in 3-quart saucepan. Add milk and butter. Place over medium-high heat, stirring constantly. Bring to full, rolling boil. Continue cooking, stirring occasionally and gradually lowering temperature of mixture to 234°. Remove from heat; add vanilla. Beat candy in pan with wooden spoon. Sugar crystals will form as spoon scrapes against bottom of pan. Beat until candy thickens and begins to hold shape. Quickly blend in nuts. Pat into an 8-inch square pan. Cut while warm.

Corn Syrup Fudge

1 pound sweet chocolate
3/4 cup corn syrup, less 2 tablespoons
Flavoring
Food color

Melt chocolate and blend in corn syrup. Add flavor and color as desired. Use yellow coating and lemon oil for lemon fudge, orange coating and oil for orange fudge. **NOTE:** Milk chocolate, light chocolate-flavored coating or colored coatings may be used.

Rich Chocolate Fudge

3-1/2 cups granulated sugar
1-1/2 cups semi-sweet chocolate wafers
3/4 cup whipping cream
3/4 cup whole milk
1/4 teaspoon salt
1 tablespoon corn syrup
6 tablespoons butter
1 teaspoon vanilla
2 cups chopped walnuts

In a 3-quart saucepan combine sugar, chocolate, cream, milk, salt and corn syrup. Cook over medium heat; stir occasionally until chocolate melts. Turn heat to medium-high, bring to full, rolling boil. Gradually lower heat as mixture thickens; stir very little. Cook to 235°. Remove from heat, add butter; let cool until warm. Add vanilla. Beat until mixture loses gloss and begins to cream. When nearly set up, blend in nuts. Spread in buttered 9-inch square pan. **NOTE:** If cooling fudge on marble slab, cut butter into small pieces. Place on slab and pour hot candy over them. As candy cools, butter will soften and can be worked in as it is creamed.

Quick Honey Fudge

1 pound sweet chocolate
3/4 cup honey, less 2 tablespoons

Melt chocolate and add honey, blending thoroughly. Pat into buttered 6-inch square pan or small loaf pan; let set. Cut into squares. **NOTE:** Either milk chocolate or light chocolate-flavored wafers may be used.

Burnt Sugar Fudge

4 cups granulated sugar
2 cups half and half cream
2 cups granulated sugar, melted
1/4 teaspoon baking soda
1/2 cup butter
6 cups chopped pecans

In a heavy 4-quart saucepan combine 4 cups sugar and cream. Bring to a boil. In heavy 10-inch skillet over medium heat melt 2 cups sugar. Stir sugar constantly. First it will turn to small, hard lumps, then will dissolve into liquid sugar. Stir constantly. Do not let sugar cook beyond light golden color. When sugar is almost melted, remove from heat. Stir until all lumps are melted. Carefully pour one-third of cream and sugar mixture into melted sugar. Return to heat. Bring to full boil. Continue cooking until ingredients are blended. Pour mixture back into remainder of cream and sugar. Stir constantly. Continue cooking until mixture reaches 246°. Remove from heat; add baking soda and butter. Stir; let set for 30 minutes. Blend in nuts. Pour into buttered 9-inch square pan. Cut into pieces while slightly warm.

Coconut Fudge

2 cups light brown sugar, firmly packed
2 cups granulated sugar
1/4 cup light corn syrup
2/3 cup whole milk
2/3 cup whipping cream
1/4 teaspoon salt
1/4 cup butter
1 teaspoon vanilla
1-1/2 cups flaked coconut, finely chopped

In a heavy 3-quart saucepan, combine sugars, corn syrup, milk, cream and salt. Cook on medium-high heat, stirring occasionally. Gradually lower heat until mixture thickens and reaches 238°. Remove from heat, pour immediately into mixer bowl. Add butter without stirring. Do not scrape pan into bowl. Place thermometer in candy; cool to 120°. Mix at lowest speed of mixer, watching candy carefully. When candy begins to cream and loses gloss, stop beater and mix by hand. Add vanilla and chopped coconut. Spread candy in a buttered 8-inch square pan. Cut into squares.

Maple Fudge

1/2 cup butter, melted
3-3/4 cups brown sugar, divided
1-1/2 cups half and half cream
2 tablespoons corn syrup
1/4 teaspoon salt
1 teaspoon maple flavoring, optional
1/4 teaspoon pecan flavoring
1-1/2 cups chopped pecans

Melt butter in heavy 3-quart saucepan. Add 1-3/4 cups brown sugar; blend into butter. Stir gently until sugar and butter are bubbling. Carefully add cream. While stirring, add the rest of brown sugar, corn syrup and salt. Stir until blended. Cook, stirring occasionally until mixture reaches 238°. Gradually lower heat as mixture thickens. Cool until lukewarm. Add flavorings, beat until creamy. When nearly set up, blend in nuts. Spread into buttered 9-inch square pan.

Party Fudge

3 cups brown sugar
1 cup whole milk
1/4 cup butter
1/4 teaspoon cream of tartar
1/4 teaspoon salt
2 cups marshmallow cream
1-3/4 cups semi-sweet chocolate coating
1-3/4 cups butterscotch coating
1-1/2 cups chopped walnuts OR pecans
1 teaspoon vanilla

In a heavy 4-quart saucepan combine sugar, milk, butter, cream of tartar and salt. Cook to 234°, stirring occasionally. Gradually lower heat as candy thickens. Remove from heat. Add remaining ingredients. Stir to melt coatings. Pour into a buttered 13- x 9- x 2-inch pan. **NOTE:** Either wafers or finely chopped block chocolate-flavored coating may be used.

Quick Peanut Butter Fudge

2 pounds peanut butter coating OR butterscotch
   coating
3/4 cup honey
1 cup peanut butter
1 cup chopped peanuts

Melt coating. Blend in honey, peanut butter and chopped peanuts. Spread into a 9-inch square pan. Let set; cut into squares.

Banana-Nut Fudge

2 bananas, mashed
2-1/2 cups granulated sugar
1/2 cup brown sugar
1 cup whole milk
1/2 teaspoon cream of tartar
2 tablespoons butter
1/4 teaspoon salt
1/4 teaspoon cinnamon
1/8 teaspoon cloves
1 teaspoon vanilla
1 cup chopped walnuts

Cook all ingredients except vanilla and nuts over medium heat, stirring occasionally. When mixture reaches 226°, stir constantly until it reaches 236°. Add vanilla. Beat until mixture starts to cream and loses gloss. This fudge may be beaten either by hand, with mixer or worked on cold surface. Blend in nuts. Quickly spread in buttered 8-inch square pan. Cut while slightly warm. Do not work candy too long or it will not pat evenly in pan.

Cooked Honey Fudge

3 cups granulated sugar
1/2 cup honey
1/8 teaspoon salt
1/2 teaspoon cream of tartar
1/2 cup milk
2/3 cup whipping cream
2 tablespoons butter, softened
1 teaspoon vanilla

In a heavy 4-quart saucepan combine sugar, honey, salt, cream of tartar, milk and cream. Stir to combine all ingredients. Place over medium-high heat; cook to 238°. Cool to 110°. While beating add butter and vanilla. Beat until candy is creamy and loses gloss. Pour into a 7-inch square pan. Cut into squares when set.

Brown Sugar Fudge

1 cup butter
1 pound dark brown sugar
2-1/2 cups granulated sugar
1 large can evaporated milk
2 cups (7 ounces) marshmallow cream
2 cups coarsely chopped walnuts or pecans

In a heavy 4-quart saucepan melt butter. Add sugars and milk. Cook over moderate heat. Stir constantly for 15 minutes after boiling starts. Remove from heat. Put marshmallow cream in mixer bowl; slowly add cooked candy. Continue beating 5 minutes, until well blended and creamy. Add nuts, pour into a buttered 15- x 11- x 1-inch pan. Let set up; cut into squares when completely cool.

Sour Cream Fudge

3 cups granulated sugar
1 cup sour cream
1/4 cup milk
1 tablespoon corn syrup
2 tablespoons butter
1/8 teaspoon salt
2 teaspoons vanilla
1 cup coarsely chopped pecans
16 - 20 pecan halves

In a 3-quart saucepan combine sugar, sour cream, milk, corn syrup, butter and salt. Place over medium-high heat; stir until sugar is moistened. Cook, gradually lowering heat as mixture thickens. Stir occasionally until mixture reaches 238°. Cool to lukewarm. Add vanilla. Beat until candy becomes creamy and holds shape. Quickly blend in nuts and spread in an 8-inch square pan. Mark into squares and press pecan half into top of each square.

Chocolate Molasses Fudge

2 cups granulated sugar
1 cup light brown sugar
3/8 cup light molasses
1/2 cup whole milk
1/4 cup whipping cream
1 cup semi-sweet chocolate wafers
4 tablespoons butter
1/2 teaspoon cream of tartar
1/4 teaspoon salt
2 teaspoons vanilla

In a heavy 3-quart saucepan place all ingredients except vanilla. Place over medium heat. Stir until chocolate melts and sugar is dissolved. Cook without stirring to 238°. Remove from heat; pour on marble slab or cold surface. When candy reaches 110°, work with fondant paddle until creamy and loses gloss. Add vanilla while working candy. Scoop fudge into buttered 8-inch pan. Let set up. Cut into squares while warm.

Low Cholesterol Cocoa Fudge

4 cups granulated sugar
3/4 cup cocoa
1/4 teaspoon salt, optional
2 cups skim milk
1 cup corn oil margarine
2 teaspoons vanilla
1-1/2 cups walnuts, optional

In heavy 4-quart saucepan mix together sugar, cocoa and salt. Add milk and margarine. Cook over medium-high heat, stirring occasionally. When mixture reaches 235°, remove from heat. Cool to 110°-115°. When candy has cooled; beat or work it. Add vanilla. Beat until creamy and mixture begins to hold shape. Scoop into a buttered 9-inch square pan. When fudge sets up but is still warm, cut into squares. Add nuts as candy gets creamy. **NOTE:** Cooling fudge may be done in pan, taking a couple of hours or on marble slab, taking a few minutes.

Cherry Fudge

3 cups granulated sugar
1/2 cup butter
1/2 cup half and half cream
1/2 cup whole milk
1/8 teaspoon salt
1-1/4 cups white coating
1-1/4 cups pink coating
2-1/2 cups miniature marshmallows
1/2 teaspoon vanilla
1/8 teaspoon concentrated cherry flavoring
1/2 cup finely chopped candied cherries
  (not maraschino)

In a 3-quart saucepan combine sugar, butter cream, milk and salt. Stir until all sugar is moistened. Cook over medium-high heat until mixture reaches 238°. Stir occasionally. Remove from heat and immediately add coatings, marshmallows, vanilla, cherry flavoring and candied cherries. Stir until ingredients are thoroughly blended into cooked candy. Spread into a 9-inch square pan. Cut into squares when set up.

Peanut Butter Fudge

3 cups granulated sugar
1/2 cup butter
2/3 cup evaporated milk
1-1/2 cups butterscotch coating
2 cups marshmallow cream
1 cup crunchy peanut butter
1 teaspoon vanilla

In a heavy 3-quart saucepan combine sugar, butter and milk. Cook over medium heat. Bring to full boil, stirring constantly. Boil 5 minutes. Remove from heat, add the rest of ingredients. Stir together and pour into a buttered 13- x 9- x 2-inch pan. Cut into squares when cool.

Facts About Fudge

The word "fudge" conjures up memories of delightful sessions with the family in the kitchen where the tempting sweet aroma of the cooking candy heightened everyone's expectations of the treat.

In earlier times, making fudge required hard beating. While in many fudges mixing in some form is still necessary, there are easier ways to get the same results. Most recipes require beating the fudge, using these three methods:

1. After cooling the mixture in the pan, which may take several hours, beat the fudge with a wooden spoon until creamy.

2. Immediately after removing the caked fudge from the heat, pour the fudge into a mixing bowl to cool. The thermometer can be left in the candy. When cooled, mix at the lowest speed of the mixer. When the fudge begins to get creamy, stop mixer and finish beating with a wooden spoon until smooth.

3. Remove the fudge from heat and pour on a marble slab or other cold surface to cool quickly. Scrape around the edges and into the center of the candy, then work the entire batch. Work the candy as quickly as possible. When the candy begins to cream, add nuts and scoop into a prepared pan.

Almost Candy

Peanut Butter-Chocolate Bars

2 eggs
1 cup sugar
1/2 teaspoon vanilla
1 cup flour
1 teaspoon baking powder
1/4 teaspoon salt
1/2 cup milk
1-1/2 tablespoons butter
3/4 cup peanut butter
2 cups white coating, melted
2 cups sweet chocolate-flavored coating, melted
1-1/2 tablespoons paramount crystals OR corn oil

Beat eggs until very light and thick. Slowly add sugar. Mix in vanilla. Add flour, baking powder and salt. Heat milk and butter; do not boil. Add to batter. Pour into a greased 13- x 9- x 2-inch pan. Bake in a 350° oven for 25 to 30 minutes. Let baked cake cool 5 minutes. Melt peanut butter and white coating; spread on cake. Melt sweet chocolate; add crystals or oil. Spread over peanut butter mixture. Let cool and set up. Cut into bars.

Fudge Filled Peanut Butter Bars

1 cup semi-sweet chocolate wafers
1 14-ounce can sweetened condensed milk
1/4 cup peanut butter
3/4 cup butter, softened
1/3 cup peanut butter
1/4 teaspoon salt
1 cup confectioners' sugar
1-1/2 cups flour
1 cup quick oats

Melt chocolate over hot water. Add sweetened condensed milk and 1/4 cup peanut butter; blend. Set aside. Beat butter, 1/3 cup peanut butter, salt and confectioners' sugar until smooth. Add flour and oats; blend. Save 1 cup of oats and press remainder in a 13- x 9- x 2-inch pan. Spread chocolate mixture over crumb mixture. Crumble remaining oats mixture evenly over top; press down gently. Bake at 350° for 30 minutes or until top crumbs are lightly browned. Cool; cut into bars.

Hazelnut Florentines

1-1/4 cups ground hazelnuts, roasted
1 cup granulated sugar
2/3 cup egg whites
2 tablespoons corn syrup
1/8 teaspoon salt
1/8 teaspoon cinnamon
1/3 cup finely chopped candied cherries and pineapple
1/2 cup flour
1/4 teaspoon baking powder
Semi-sweet chocolate, melted

Mix ingredients together. Drop by teaspoonsful, 2 inches apart on heavily greased cookie sheet. Bake at 350° for 8 to 12 minutes or until light browned and crisp on edges. Remove immediately. When cool, spread melted chocolate on bottoms of cookies.

Peanut Butter Surprises

1/2 cup butter
1/2 cup granulated sugar
1/2 cup brown sugar
2/3 cup peanut butter
1 egg
1/2 teaspoon vanilla
1 cup flour
1/4 teaspoon salt
3/4 teaspoon baking soda
55 to 60 sweet chocolate wafers

Beat butter, sugars, peanut butter, egg and vanilla until light and fluffy. Add flour, salt and baking soda. Form into 1-inch balls. Flatten slightly with fork and place a wafer in center. Stretch dough around wafer, completely concealing it. Place cookies on ungreased cookie sheet. Mark lightly both ways with fork. Bake at 350° for 10 to 12 minutes or until set and very lightly browned on edges. Makes about 55 to 60 cookies.

Chewy Double Chocolate Chippers

Cookies:
2/3 cup butter
1/2 cup granulated sugar
1/2 cup brown sugar
1 egg
1/4 teaspoon invert sugar*
1 teaspoon vanilla
1-3/4 cups flour
1/2 teaspoon salt
1/2 teaspoon baking soda
1 cup semi-sweet chocolate chips

Frosting:
1-1/2 cups dry fondant
2 tablespoons cocoa
2 tablespoons butter
Pinch salt
1/2 teaspoon vanilla
2 tablespoons milk

*Recipe for invert sugar is on page 52. **Cookies:** Beat butter, sugars, egg, invert sugar and vanilla. Add dry ingredients and beat. Blend in chocolate. Drop by tablespoons on ungreased cookie sheet. Bake at 350° for 15 to 18 minutes. Let partially cool; frost. **Frosting:** Beat all ingredients. Spread on cookies while warm.

Lemon Tartlets

Pastry:
1/2 cup butter
1 cup flour
1 3-ounce package cream cheese

Filling:
2 egg yolks
2 tablespoons butter, softened
1 tablespoon lemon juice
3/4 tablespoon lemon rind
1 tablespoon water
1/2 cup sugar

Pastry: Combine 1/2 cup butter, flour and cream cheese with pastry blender or mixer. Turn out on lightly floured surface. Form into long roll. Divide roll into 24 equal parts. Roll each part into a ball, place in miniature cupcake pans. With fingers, line cavities of cupcake pans with pastry. **Filling:** Break egg yolks together with fork. Beat in butter, lemon juice, rind and water. Stir in sugar. Spoon scant 1/2 teaspoon filling into each cavity. Bake at 375° for 25 minutes. Let stand

in pan 5 minutes; carefully remove to wire rack. Filling becomes thicker as it cools. Makes 24 tartlets.

Pecan Tartlets

Pastry:
1/2 cup butter
1 cup flour
1 3-ounce package cream cheese

Filling:
1 egg
1 tablespoon butter, softened
1 tablespoon corn syrup
2/3 cup brown sugar
Pinch of salt
1 egg yolk
1/2 teaspoon vanilla
1/2 cup finely chopped pecans
24 pecan halves

Pastry: Combine 1/2 cup butter, flour and cream cheese with pastry blender or mixer. Turn out on lightly floured surface. Form into long roll. Divide roll into 24 equal parts. Roll each part into a ball, place in miniature cupcake pans. With fingers, line cavities of cupcake pans with pastry. **Filling:** Beat together egg, 1 tablespoon butter, corn syrup, sugar, salt, egg yolk and vanilla. Add chopped pecans. Fill pastry shells. Place pecan half on each. Bake at 325° for 25 minutes. Makes 24 tartlets.

Chocolate Chip Bar Cookies

3/4 cup granulated sugar
3/4 cup brown sugar
1 cup butter
2 eggs
1 teaspoon vanilla
1-1/4 cups flour
1 teaspoon baking soda
1 teaspoon salt
2 cups semi-sweet chocolate pieces, chopped
1 cup chopped nuts, optional

Beat sugars, butter, eggs and vanilla until light and creamy. Sift flour, soda and salt. Blend in chocolate and nuts. Spread in buttered 13- x 9- x 2-inch pan. Bake in a 350° oven for 25 to 30 minutes or until golden brown. May be frosted with chocolate icing, if desired.

Oatmeal Chocolate Chunkies

1/2 cup butter
1/2 cup vegetable shortening
1 cup brown sugar
1 cup granulated sugar
2 eggs
1 teaspoon vanilla
1-1/2 cups flour
1 teaspoon salt
1 teaspoon baking soda
3 cups quick oats
1 cup semi-sweet wafers, coarsely chopped

Cream together butter, shortening and sugars. Add eggs and vanilla. Beat until light and fluffy. Stir in flour, salt and soda. Blend in oats and chopped chocolate. Drop by tablespoons on ungreased cookie sheet. Bake in a 350° oven for 15 to 18 minutes or until golden brown.

Seven Layer Cookies

1/3 cup butter
1 cup graham cracker crumbs, about 16 squares
1 cup butterscotch wafers
1 cup semi-sweet chocolate wafers
3/4 cup flaked coconut
1 cup chopped nuts
1 14-ounce can condensed milk

Melt butter in an 8-inch square pan. Sprinkle cracker crumbs over butter. In layers add ingredients in order listed. Pour sweetened condensed milk over all ingredients. Bake at 350° for 30 minutes. Cut into bars or squares when cool.

Mexican Dessert Candy

12 egg yolks
1 cup sugar
2 cups sifted flour
1 cup milk
2 lime rinds, grated
1/2 cup butter, cut into small pieces
2 tablespoons confectioners' sugar
1 teaspoon cinnamon

Beat egg yolks slightly. Mix sugar and flour. Add milk and sugar-flour mixture alternately to egg yolks. Mix thoroughly at slow speed after each addition. Add grated rinds; mix. Pour into heavy 3-quart saucepan. Add butter. Cook over moderate-low heat until mixture is very thick. Pour into a 13- x 9- x 2-inch pan; cool. Cut into 1-1/4- x 1-inch strips. Deep fry until lightly browned. Drain on paper toweling. When slightly cooled, roll in mixture of cinnamon and sugar.

Butterscotch-Chocolate Bars

1 cup butter
1 cup brown sugar
1 egg yolk
1 teaspoon vanilla
2 cups flour
1 cup sweet chocolate wafers
3/4 cup finely chopped pecans

Combine butter, sugar, egg and vanilla. Add flour. Spread in a 13- x 9- x 2-inch buttered pan. Bake at 350° for 20 to 25 minutes. Remove from oven. Immediately place wafers evenly over hot dough. Let set until chocolate softens. Spread evenly with spatula. Sprinkle nuts over soft chocolate; let set up. Cut into small bars.

Party Cookies

Cookies:
1 cup butter
1/2 cup brown sugar
1/4 cup granulated sugar
1 egg yolk
1/2 teaspoon vanilla
2 cups flour
1/8 teaspoon salt

Icing:
1 cup confectioners' sugar
Pinch salt
1/4 teaspoon vanilla
1 tablespoon butter
1-1/2 tablespoons milk
Food coloring, optional

Cookies: Cream butter and sugars together until light and fluffy. Add egg yolk and vanilla; beat smooth. Blend in flour and salt. Form into small balls; flatten slightly. Bake in 375° oven for 8 to 10 minutes on ungreased cookie sheet. When nearly cool, frost with icing. **Icing:** Mix ingredients together. Beat until smooth.

Shown on opposite page: Corn Flake Chews, Peanut Butter Surprises, Oatmeal Chocolate Chunkies, Top of the Stove Date Balls, Party Cookies, Pecan Tartlets.

Mother Brand's Peanut Cookies

2 eggs
1 cup brown sugar
1/2 cup sifted flour
1/2 teaspoon baking powder
1/4 teaspoon cinnamon
Pinch salt
2/3 cup finely chopped peanuts

Stir eggs in bowl by hand, not mixer. Add sugar, flour, baking powder, cinnamon and salt. Mix just to blend. Stir in peanuts. Spread in buttered 8-inch square pan. Bake at 350° for 10 to 12 minutes. Cut while warm.

Chewy Chocolate Brownies

Brownies:
2 ounces baking chocolate
1/3 cup vegetable shortening OR butter
1 cup granulated sugar
2 eggs
3/4 cup flour
1/2 teaspoon baking powder
1/2 teaspoon salt
3/4 cup chopped pecans OR walnuts, optional

Icing:
1-1/2 cups confectioners' sugar
1/2 teaspoon vanilla
Pinch salt
2 tablespoons butter
1-1/2 tablespoons cocoa
3 to 3-1/2 tablespoons milk
Pecans OR walnuts, optional

Brownies: Melt chocolate and shortening over medium heat; stir constantly. Remove from heat; beat in sugar. Add eggs, one at a time, beating by hand after each addition. Blend in flour, baking powder and salt. Add nuts. Spread in buttered 8-inch square pan. Bake in a 350° oven for 30 to 35 minutes. Cool and spread with chocolate icing. **Icing:** Beat ingredients together until spreadable consistency. Spread over cooled cookies and sprinkle chopped pecans or walnuts over soft icing.

Black Walnut Slices

Cookies:
3 eggs
1/2 cup granulated sugar
2 cups flour, unsifted
1-1/4 teaspoons baking powder
1 cup semi-sweet chocolate wafers, melted
1 cup black walnuts
1/2 cup chopped almonds

Icing:
1 cup confectioners' sugar
1/4 teaspoon vanilla
Pinch salt
1 tablespoon butter
1 tablespoon cocoa
2-1/2 tablespoons milk

Cookies: Beat eggs and sugar. Add flour and baking powder. Blend in melted chocolate. Add nuts. Turn out on floured surface; knead smooth. Divide into 4 parts; roll each into logs 1-inch wide. Bake at 350° for 15 minutes; let cool, slice and frost. **Icing:** In small mixing bowl combine sugar, vanilla, salt, butter and cocoa. Add 1-1/2 tablespoons milk; beat smooth. Gradually add the rest of liquid until spreadable consistency.

Corn Flake Chews

2-1/2 cups brown sugar
3/4 cup butter
1 cup desiccated OR macaroon coconut
2 cups walnuts
3 eggs
2 teaspoons vanilla
8-1/2 cups corn flakes

Cream sugar and butter. Add coconut, nuts, eggs and vanilla; beat. Stir in corn flakes. Drop on buttered cookie sheet, 2 inches apart. Bake at 375° for 8 to 10 mintes or until golden brown. Remove from oven. Let set 3 to 4 minutes. Makes about 60 cookies.

Shown on opposite page: Coconut Squares, Peanut Patties, Fudgy Rocky Road Drops, Chocolate Pralines, Coconut Fruit Balls, Chewy Peanut Candy.

Best-Tasting Brittle

Sparkling Rock Candy

1-3/4 cups granulated sugar
1/2 cup water
1/2 cup light corn syrup
1/8 teaspoon salt
Food coloring
Flavoring oil
Confectioners' sugar

In small saucepan combine sugar, water, corn syrup and salt. Cover tightly. Cook until steam comes from under lid. Remove lid, insert thermometer. Cook to 250°. Add food coloring. Cook to 290°. Remove from heat. Let cool 5 minutes. Add flavoring oil; cover 5 minutes. Remove lid, stir to blend in flavoring. Pour into an 11- x 7- x 1-1/2-inch buttered pan. When candy is cool enough to handle, start cutting narrow strips from edges. Work around pan. As each strip is cut, cut off smaller pieces from it. Dust with confectioners' sugar. Without sugar, candy will look like stained glass. Store in airtight container to prevent stickiness. Hot candy may be poured in buttered metal molds, in rubber sucker molds or spooned on buttered cookie sheet into desired shapes.

Deluxe Nuts Supreme

3-4 cups deluxe nuts, without peanuts
2 cups granulated sugar
1/3 cup light corn syrup
1/2 teaspoon salt
1 cup butter
1 teaspoon baking soda
1 teaspoon vanilla

Keep nuts warm in 200° oven. In heavy 3-quart saucepan mix sugar, corn syrup and salt. Bring to boil over high heat. Stir constantly. Mixture will be thick. Continue cooking. Stir until mixture reaches 310°. If ball of thermometer is not covered by cooking syrup, tip pan to get accurate reading. Add butter, continue to stir. Butter will stay on top of cooking syrup. Cook to high, rolling boil, about 290°. Syrup will be light golden brown. Remove from stove. Stir in baking soda and vanilla. Add warm nuts. Stir to coat. Pour on buttered marble slab or cookie sheet. After 5 minutes, turn candy over and stretch candy to even thickness. Candy will be hot. Let set and break into pieces.

Peanut Butter Brittle

1 cup peanut butter
1 tablespoon butter
1/2 teaspoon vanilla
1/8 teaspoon salt
1 cup granulated sugar
1/3 cup light corn syrup
1/3 cup water

In a double boiler heat peanut butter, butter, vanilla and salt. In a separate saucepan combine sugar, corn syrup and water. Cook to 305°. Remove from heat. Add warm peanut butter mixture; stir until completely blended. Immediately pour into a buttered 15- x 11- x 1-inch pan. Spread as thinly as possible. When cool, break into pieces.

Almond Toffee

1 cup coarsely chopped almonds
1 cup butter
1 cup granulated sugar
1/2 cup light brown sugar
1 tablespoon light corn syrup
3 tablespoons water
1/2 teaspoon lecithin

Warm almonds in 200° oven. Melt butter in 2-quart saucepan. Add sugars, corn syrup, water and lecithin. Cook to 275°, stirring frequently. Add hot almonds. Continue cooking to 300°; stir constantly. Pour on well buttered surface. Turn slab of candy over after 3 minutes. Turn again in 5 minutes. Allow candy to cool. **NOTE:** Toffee may be dipped in tempered real chocolate.

Dark Toffee

2 cups light brown sugar
1 cup dark corn syrup
1 cup butter
1/2 teaspoon lecithin
1 teaspoon vanilla

In heavy 3-quart saucepan combine brown sugar, corn syrup, butter and lecithin. Stir occasionally. Cook to 290°. Gradually lower heat as mixture thickens. Remove from heat, add vanilla. Pour on heavily buttered surface, turning several times while cooling.

Coconut Brittle

1 cup sugar
1 cup boiling water
2 cups sugar
1-3/4 cups light corn syrup
3 tablespoons butter
1 teaspoon salt
1-3/4 cups salted roasted peanuts
4 cups raw chip coconut

In heavy 4-quart saucepan place 1 cup sugar. Place over high heat. Stir constantly until sugar dissolves and turns light golden brown. Do not let sugar become too dark or it will be scorched. Add boiling water to melted sugar. Mixture will steam. Melted sugar will form soft lump. Let mixture boil until lump dissolves. Add remaining 2 cups sugar and corn syrup. Cook to 295°. Remove from heat. Add butter and salt; stir until dissolved. Quickly stir in peanuts and coconut. Turn out on buttered marble slab or well buttered cookie sheet. Spread thinly as possible. Turn over after 3 minutes. Stretch so candy is even thickness. Cool completely. Break into small pieces. Store in airtight containers.

Butterscotch Squares Or Patties

2 cups granulated sugar
1/4 teaspoon salt
1/4 cup light corn syrup
1/4 cup honey
1/2 cup butter
2 tablespoons vinegar
2 tablespoons water
Egg yellow food coloring
4 drops butter flavoring

In a heavy 3-quart saucepan combine sugar, salt, corn syrup, honey, butter, vinegar and water. Place over high heat. Stir until mixture is well blended and starts to cook. Cook to 250°. add coloring as mixture boils. Cook to 300°; stir occasionally. Gradually lower heat. Remove from heat, stir in butter flavoring. Pour into buttered miniature cupcake pans or on generously buttered cookie sheet. Remove patties almost immediately. Patties are difficult to remove if allowed to completely cool in pans. If pouring candy on buttered cookie sheet, score when it begins to cool, score again in 3 minutes. Break on scored marks when completely cool.

Butter Pecan Toffee

1 cup butter
1 cup sugar
1/4 teaspoon salt
3 tablespoons water
1/2 teaspoon lecithin
1/2 cup finely chopped pecans

Melt butter. Stir in sugar, salt, water and lecithin. Cook to 290° stirring occasionally. Quickly stir in nuts. Pour on large buttered cookie sheet. When cool, break into pieces.

Peanut Brittle

1 cup granulated sugar
1 cup light brown sugar
1 cup light corn syrup
3/4 cup water
3 cups raw peanuts
2 tablespoons butter
1 teaspoon baking soda
1 teaspoon salt

In a 3-quart saucepan combine sugars, corn syrup and water. Cover tightly. Cook until steam comes from under lid. Remove lid, insert thermometer. Cook to 240°. Add peanuts. Cook to 295°; stir constantly. Remove from heat, add butter. Mix in soda and salt; stir vigorously. Pour on buttered marble slab or buttered cookie sheet. Spread thinly as possible. Let set 5 minutes. Turn candy over. Pull small pieces as thin as possible. Candy will be very hot.

Glazed Deluxe Nuts

1 12-ounce can deluxe mixed nuts
1-1/2 cups granulated sugar
1 cup light corn syrup
1/3 cup water
1/2 teaspoon salt
2 tablespoons butter
1 teaspoon vanilla

Spread nuts in pan and heat in 225° oven. Combine sugar, corn syrup, water and salt in a 3-quart saucepan. Cover and cook until steam comes from under lid. Remove lid and insert thermometer; cook to 295°. Remove from heat, stir in warm nuts, butter and vanilla. Spread coated nuts on generously buttered marble slab or 2 well buttered cookie sheets. After a few minutes turn candy over. Spread and pull until nuts are single thickness and syrup between nuts is pulled thin. Cool completely; break into pieces.

Chocolate Coated Butter Brickle

1 cup finely chopped pecans
1 cup butter
2 cups granulated sugar
6 tablespoons hot water
1/2 teaspoon cream of tartar
1/2 teaspoon salt
1-1/4 pounds real milk chocolate, tempered
3/4 cup finely chopped pecans

Warm 1 cup pecans in 200° oven. In heavy 2-quart saucepan melt butter. Add sugar, water, cream of tartar and salt. Cook to 280°. Add warm pecans, stirring constantly. Cook to 305°. Pour on well buttered surface. Turn several times as candy cools. When completely cool, spread with chocolate; let set up. When chocolate sets, turn candy over on waxed paper. Coat other side with chocolate. Sprinkle nuts over soft chocolate.

Filbert Brittle

2-1/2 cups granulated sugar
3/4 cup light corn syrup
1/4 teaspoon salt
3/4 cup water
5 tablespoons butter
3 cups raw filbert nuts
1 teaspoon baking soda
1 teaspoon vanilla

In a heavy 3-quart saucepan combine sugar, corn syrup, salt, water and butter. Cook to 250°, stir occasionally. Remove skins and stems from filberts. Add to syrup mixture. Cook to 210°, stir constantly. Remove from heat. Add baking soda and vanilla. Stir thoroughly. Spread on buttered surface. After 5 minutes, turn candy over to cool bottom. When completely cool, break into pieces. Store in airtight containers.

Crunchy Golden Brittle

2-1/2 cups sugar
1/4 cup light brown sugar
1 cup water
1/2 teaspoon cream of tartar
1/4 cup dark corn syrup
1 teaspoon baking soda
2 teaspoons water

In a 3-quart saucepan mix sugars, water, cream of tartar and corn syrup over high heat. Stir to dissolve sugar. Cook to 310°, stirring occasionally. Dissolve baking soda in 2 teaspoons water. Remove cooked candy from heat and stir in soda mixture. Pour on buttered surface; let cool. Break into pieces. Store in airtight container.

Crisp Peanut Caramel Corn

1 cup granulated sugar
2 cups light brown sugar
1 cup water
4 tablespoons light corn syrup
1 teaspoon salt
2 tablespoons butter
6 quarts popped corn
3 cups roasted peanuts

In a 3-quart saucepan combine sugars, water, corn syrup and salt. Stir until boiling starts. Cover; watch closely. Remove lid when sugar is dissolved. Insert thermometer. Cook, without stirring to 285°. Remove from heat; add butter. Stir until melted. Place corn and peanuts in large buttered bowl. Pour hot syrup over, stirring well. Turn coated popcorn and nuts out on two buttered cookie sheets or buttered marble slab. When cool, break into pieces.

Popcorn Squares

2 cups granulated sugar
1/2 cup light corn syrup
1/2 cup invert sugar*
1 cup water
1/2 teaspoon salt
1 teaspoon vinegar
3 tablespoons butter
1 teaspoon vanilla
5 quarts popped corn

*Recipe for invert sugar is on page 52. In a 2-quart saucepan combine sugar, corn syrup, invert sugar, water, salt and vinegar. Cover tightly; cook until sugar dissolves. Remove lid, insert thermometer. Cook to 265°; remove from heat. Add butter and vanilla; stir. Put popped corn in large buttered bowl. Pour cooked syrup over popcorn, stirring to coat. Dampen hands and shape popcorn into rectangle, about 1 inch thick. Press down firmly. Let cool. Cut into squares and wrap each in waxed paper or plastic film.

Shown on opposite page: Spiced Nuts, Crisp Peanut Caramel Corn, Glazed Deluxe Nuts, Popcorn Squares, Crunchy Golden Brittle, Almond Toffee, Filbert Brittle, Chocolate Coated Butter Brickle.

Creamy Caramels

Special Caramels

2-1/2 cups granulated sugar
2 cups whipping cream
1-1/4 cups light corn syrup
1/2 cup butter
2 tablespoons invert sugar*, optional
2 cups hot whipping cream
1 14-ounce can sweetened condensed milk

*Recipe for invert sugar is on page 52. In a heavy 6-quart dutch oven combine sugar, 2 cups whipping cream, corn syrup, butter and invert sugar. Place over high heat; bring to boil. Boil rapidly 2 minutes. Add hot cream very slowly. Continue cooking rapidly for 2 more minutes. Stir very little. Add sweetened condensed milk very slowly. Keep it boiling; stir constantly. Cook until mixture reaches 242°. Stir in circular motion to reach every portion of pan. Lower heat gradually as candy thickens, about 25 minutes. Pour candy in 13- x 9- x 2-inch pan lined with foil and greased. Let cool. Cut into squares and wrap in clear plastic film or dip in chocolate, if desired.

Chocolate Caramel Pinwheels

Chocolate Caramel:
1 cup granulated sugar
1/2 cup light corn syrup
1-1/2 tablespoons light molasses
1 ounce baking chocolate
1/8 teaspoon salt
1 tablespoon invert sugar*
3 tablespoons butter
1/2 cup whipping cream
1/4 cup hot whipping cream
1/2 teaspoon vanilla

Coconut Filling:
18 large marshmallows
3/4 cup corn syrup
3 cups desiccated OR macaroon coconut
1-1/2 teaspoons vanilla

*Recipe for invert sugar is on page 52.
Chocolate Caramel: In a 2-quart saucepan combine sugar, corn syrup, molasses, chocolate, salt, invert sugar, butter and 1/2 cup whipping cream. Place over medium heat. Stir until chocolate melts and sugar dissolves. Raise heat to medium-high; boil rapidly for 1-1/2 minutes. Very slowly add HOT cream. Continue cooking until mixture reaches 247°. Add vanilla. Pour in foil-lined 13- x 9- x 2-inch, greased pan. Let cool. **Coconut Filling:** Melt marshmallows in corn syrup over medium heat. Remove from stove; add coconut and vanilla. Let cool. Remove cooled caramel from pan, peel off foil. Spread coconut filling over chocolate caramel. Roll tightly, starting at wide side. Stretch roll to desired size. Slice pinwheels. Wrap each in clear plastic film or dip each in chocolate. **NOTE:** 1/2 cup semi-sweet chocolate wafers may be used in place of 1 ounce baking chocolate.

Reduced Cholesterol Caramels

2 cups granulated sugar
1/2 cup light brown sugar
1 cup light corn syrup
1 can Milnot
1/4 cup invert sugar*
1/2 cup corn oil margarine
1/4 teaspoon salt
1 teaspoon liquid lecithin
1 teaspoon vanilla
Walnuts, optional

*Recipe for invert sugar is on page 52. In a 3-quart saucepan combine sugars, corn syrup, Milnot, invert sugar, margarine and salt. Mix well. Place over medium-high heat. Beat with whisk beater as cooking starts. Continue whisking to 220°. Insert thermometer. Continue cooking, stirring frequently. When mixture reaches 240°, add lecithin; continue cooking. Stir to 246°. Just before removing from heat, add vanilla. Pour in a buttered 9-inch square pan. Cool. Cut into squares, wrap in clear plastic film. **NOTE:** Lack of stirring may cause brown spots in candy. It will not affect taste. Walnuts may be added to cover spots.

Shown on opposite page: Honey Caramel, Chocolate Caramel Pinwheels, Burnt Sugar Pecan Caramels, Molasses Delights, Vanilla Caramel.

Honey Caramels

2-1/2 cups granulated sugar
1/4 teaspoon salt
1/4 pound comb honey
3/4 cup light corn syrup
1 cup whipping cream
1/4 cup butter
1 teaspoon vanilla

In a 3-quart saucepan combine sugar, salt, honey, corn syrup, cream and butter. Stir to mix well. Place over high heat. Stir until sugar is dissolved and ingredients are blended. Continue cooking; stir occasionally. Lower heat and cook until mixture reaches 248°. Just before removing from heat, add vanilla. Stir to mix. Pour into an 8-inch square pan. Let cool. Cut into squares and wrap in clear plastic film.

Penny's Time Saving Caramels

1 cup butter
1-1/4 cups brown sugar, packed
1/8 teaspoon salt
1 cup light corn syrup
1 14-ounce can sweetened condensed milk
1 teaspoon vanilla

Melt butter in 2-quart saucepan. Stir in sugar and salt; bring to boil. Add corn syrup; bring to boil. Add sweetened condensed milk; stir constantly. Cook until mixture reaches 245°. Remove from heat, add vanilla. Pour into greased 8-inch square pan; cool. Cut in squares, wrap in plastic film.

Butterscotch Caramels

2 cups sugar
3/4 cup light brown sugar
1-2/3 cups light corn syrup
3/4 cup water
2 tablespoons cocoa butter
1/2 cup butter
1/4 teaspoon salt
1/4 cup invert sugar*
3 tablespoons whipping cream
10 drops lemon oil
8 drops butter rum concentrated flavoring
1 tablespoon paramount crystals

*Recipe for invert sugar is on page 52. In 4-quart saucepan combine sugar, brown sugar, corn syrup, water, cocoa butter, butter, salt and invert sugar. Cook on medium-high heat until mixture reaches 254°. Add whipping cream. Cook mixture to 250°; remove from heat. Add flavorings and paramount crystals; stir. Pour into a greased 9-inch square pan; cool. Cut into squares and wrap in plastic film.

Chocolate-Honey Caramels

2-1/2 cups granulated sugar
1/4 teaspoon salt
3/4 cup light corn syrup
1/4 pound comb honey
3/4 cup half and half cream
1-1/2 cups semi-sweet chocolate
1 cup hot whipping cream,
1 teaspoon vanilla

In a 3-quart saucepan combine sugar, salt, corn syrup, honey, cream and chocolate. Place over medium heat. Stir until chocolate and sugar dissolve. Turn heat to medium-high. Bring mixture to rolling boil. Let boil 2 minutes. Very slowly add hot cream. Do not let boiling stop. Continue cooking; stir occasionally, gradually lower heat until mixture reaches 248°. Before removing from heat, add vanilla. Pour into buttered 8-inch square pan. Let cool and become firm. Turn out on cutting board, cut into squares. Wrap in clear plastic film.

Old Fashioned Black Walnut Caramels

2 cups granulated sugar
1 cup light brown sugar
3/4 cup whipping cream
1 cup light corn syrup
1/2 cup butter
3/4 cup hot whipping cream
2 teaspoons vanilla
3/4 cup chopped black walnuts

In a 3-quart saucepan, combine sugars, cream, corn syrup and butter. Stir, place over medium-high heat. Cook to 230°, stirring occasionally. Add hot cream slowly. Continue to cook until mixture reaches 248°, stirring occasionally. Add vanilla just before removing from heat. Distribute walnuts over bottom of a 9-inch square pan. Pour caramel over nuts. Let cool and cut into squares. Wrap in clear plastic film or dip in milk chocolate.

Sweet and Sour Lime Caramels

2-1/2 cups granulated sugar
1/4 teaspoon salt
1 cup light corn syrup
1/4 cup water
Juice of 3 limes
6 tablespoons butter
1-1/4 cup hot whipping cream
Green food coloring

In a 3-quart saucepan combine sugar, salt, corn syrup, water, juice and butter. Bring to full boil for 1 minute or until mixture reaches 230°. Slowly dribble in hot cream. Continue cooking. Add food coloring when mixture reaches 240°. Cook to 250°. Pour in an 8-inch square pan. Cut into squares when cool and firm.

Molasses Delights

1-1/2 cups granulated sugar
1 cup light molasses
1 cup light corn syrup
1/2 cup invert sugar*
1/2 teaspoon salt
1/4 cup butter
1/2 teaspoon baking soda, sifted
Semi-sweet chocolate, optional

*Recipe for invert sugar is on page 52. In a 3-quart saucepan combine sugar, molasses, corn syrup, invert sugar, salt and butter. Cook to 255°. Remove from heat. Add soda. Mix thoroughly. Pour in a 13- x 9- x 2-inch pan. Let set up. Cut into small bars. Dip in chocolate, if desired.

Burnt Sugar Pecan Caramels

2 cups granulated sugar
1-1/2 cups whipping cream
1 cup light corn syrup
1/4 cup butter
1/4 teaspoon salt
1/2 cup granulated sugar
1/2 cup very hot water
1 teaspoon vanilla
2 cups chopped pecans

Combine 2 cups sugar, cream, corn syrup, butter and salt. In a heavy 3-quart saucepan melt 1/2 cup sugar over high heat. Stir and watch carefully. When sugar melts and turns golden brown, carefully add hot water. Sugar should not get dark brown or it will have a scorched flavor. Melted sugar will form soft lump. Boil mixture until lump dissolves; stir. Add rest of ingredients, except vanilla and pecans. Stir until 2 cups sugar are dissolved. Continue cooking until mixture reaches 246°. Add vanilla. Remove from heat; stir in nuts. Pour in an 8-inch square pan lined with foil. Foil should be greased. Let cool. Cut into squares. Wrap in clear plastic film or dip in chocolate, if desired.

Vanilla Caramels

1-1/2 cups granulated sugar
1 cup light corn syrup
1 cup whipping cream
1/2 cup butter
1/4 cup invert sugar*
1 cup hot whipping cream
1 teaspoon vanilla

*Recipe for invert sugar is on page 52. In a 3-quart saucepan combine sugar, corn syrup, whipping cream, butter and invert sugar. Bring to boil. Stir only until sugar is dissolved. When rapidly boiling, slowly add HOT whipping cream. Boiling should not stop. Continue cooking, until caramel reaches 245° for soft caramel or 250° for firm caramel. Stir very little. Just before thermometer reaches desired temperature, add vanilla. Pour into a buttered 8-inch square pan. When cool, cut into squares.

Comments About Caramels

Caramels are, by definition, a block of deliciously chewy candy. They can vary greatly in using a variety of ingredients but must always maintain their chewy consistency and never become sugary.

By using invert sugar to replace a portion of sugar, the quality of caramel is greatly improved and a good consistency is maintained.

Caramels may be cooked anywhere between 245° for a soft caramel to 252° for a very firm caramel.

To simplify the removal of caramel from a pan, line the pan with foil and butter the foil generously. The cool block of caramel can then be easily lifted from the pan and the foil removed.

Quick 'N' Easy Candy

Pecan Delights

2 pounds pecan pieces
1/2 pound caramels
Dipping chocolate

Spread nuts thickly in bottom of buttered pan. Cut caramel in small pieces and place at random over nuts, not letting caramel pieces touch. Place in 200° oven for 5 minutes or until caramel begins to melt. Remove from oven; let cool. Dip each caramel in chocolate.

Fruit Bars

4 cups miniature marshmallows
1 cup chopped walnuts
1/2 cup chopped dates
1 cup candied fruit, chopped
1 cup semi-sweet chocolate
1 cup sweet chocolate
1 can sweetened condensed milk
1 teaspoon vanilla

Combine marshmallows, nuts, dates and fruit in large bowl. Set aside. Melt chocolates. Add milk and vanilla; beat. Pour chocolate mixture over fruit and nuts and stir until well coated. Spread in buttered 9-inch square pan. Chill until firm. Cut into squares.

Quick Chocolate Fudge

5-1/2 cups dry fondant
1 14-ounce can sweetened condensed milk
1/2 teaspoon salt
1/4 cup corn syrup
1/4 cup butter
2 cups semi-sweet chocolate
1/2 cup marshmallow cream
1 teaspoon vanilla
1 cup chopped walnuts

In a heavy saucepan, heat fondant, sweetened condensed milk, salt and corn syrup over medium-low heat. Stir gently with wooden spoon. Do not let temperature get above 180°. Remove from heat. Add butter and chocolate. Stir until completely melted. Add marshmallow cream, vanilla and nuts. Pat into a buttered 13- x 9- x 2-inch pan. Cut into squares when set up.

Peanut Butter Crunch

18 ounces peanut butter
1/2 cup butter
3 cups confectioners' sugar
1 teaspoon vanilla
1/2 teaspoon salt
2-1/2 cups rice cereal
White, chocolate-flavored coating
Semi-sweet chocolate coating
Chopped peanuts

Whip peanut butter and butter. Add confectioners' sugar, vanilla and salt; mix well. Blend in rice cereal. On waxed paper, pat into a 3/8-inch thick square. Let set until firm. Cut into small bars; dip in white coating. When chocolate sets up, dip bottom of each bar in chocolate coating. Roll in chopped peanuts.

Fruit Chews

1-1/2 cups seedless raisins
1 cup dried apricots
1 cup figs
1-1/2 cups dates
1 cup orange peel
12 candied cherries
1-1/2 cups walnuts
1/4 cup orange juice
Chocolate coating, melted, optional

Process one fruit at a time in food processer or grind with course blade. Combine all fruit and nuts, making paste. Add orange juice. Roll into small balls or logs. Dip in chocolate or roll in mixture of confectioners' sugar and brown sugar.

Easy Truffles

1 pound semi-sweet chocolate
1 14-ounce can sweetened condensed milk
1/4 teaspoon butter-rum flavoring
Dipping chocolate
Chopped nuts, optional

Melt chocolate. Add sweetened condensed milk and flavoring; beat. Chill for several hours. Beat again. Roll into balls or put in pastry bag and pipe out in small mounds. Dip in chocolate. Roll on grater to achieve rough appearance. May be rolled in nuts before chocolate sets up.

Chewy Peanut Candy

1 cup peanut butter
1 cup corn syrup
1-1/4 cups dry fondant (powdered sugar may be substituted)
1-1/4 cups non-fat dry milk
1/2 cup finely chopped peanuts
Chocolate coating, melted

Blend peanut butter and corn syrup together in large bowl with mixer. Mix dry fondant and powdered milk together. Add to peanut butter and syrup a little at a time. Remove from mixer and knead by hand as mixture gets heavy. Mix in peanuts. Form into rolls. Chill and cut into 1/2 inch pieces. Dip in melted chocolate. Makes 35 pieces.

Peanut Honey Balls

1/4 cup crushed Grape Nut Flakes
3 tablespoons honey
1/4 cup peanut butter
1 teaspoon butter
1/4 cup non-fat dry milk

Set aside 2 tablespoons crushed cereal. Mix the rest of cereal with honey and peanut butter. Gradually add butter and dry milk. Blend together thoroughly. Roll into small balls. Roll each ball in reserved crushed cereal. Chill and store covered in refrigerator. Makes 14 candies.

Health Candy

4 tablespoons corn oil
1 cup condensed milk
1 teaspoon vanilla
1/8 teaspoon salt
1 cup toasted wheat germ
1 cup chopped black walnuts
1 cup raisins
1 cup dry fondant OR confectioners' sugar
1-1/2 cup non-fat dry milk
1/2 cup finely chopped black walnuts
1/2 cup crushed vanilla wafers
Semi-sweet chocolate, melted

Beat corn oil, milk and vanilla together. Blend in salt, wheat germ, walnuts and raisins. Add sugar and dry milk. Blend thoroughly; chill for 1 hour. Combine chopped walnuts and crushed wafers. Roll candy into small balls and coat with crumb mixture. Dribble on melted chocolate. Store in refrigerator. Makes 36 balls.

Fudge Sandwiches

1 cup butterscotch wafers OR pieces
1/2 cup crunchy peanut butter
1 cup miniature marshmallows
4 cups rice cereal
1 cup semi-sweet chocolate wafers
1 tablespoon paramount crystals OR corn oil
2 tablespoons marshmallow cream
1/4 cup confectioners' sugar
2 tablespoons butter

Melt butterscotch coating, add peanut butter, marshmallows and cereal. Press 1/2 of mixture in bottom of a lightly buttered 8-inch square pan. Press down with dampened fingers. Place remainder of mixture over hot water to keep warm. Melt semi-sweet coating with paramount crystals or corn oil. Add rest of ingredients at once. Beat until well blended and smooth. Drop by teaspoons over cereal layer. Pat even and smooth with damp fingers. Spread the rest of rice cereal over top. Pat smooth. Chill until firm; cut into squares.

Karin's Apriconut Balls

1-1/2 cups dried, chopped apricots
2 cups flaked coconut
2/3 cup sweetened condensed milk
3/4 cup sweet chocolate coating, melted

Grind apricots in food processer or run through food grinder. Mix finely chopped apricots with coconut. Blend sweetened condensed milk into mixture. Moisten hands and form into small balls; place on waxed paper. Melt coating, dribble over balls. Place in paper candy cups.

Date Bars

1/2 cup butter
4 cups miniature marshmallows
1/4 cup milk
2 cups sweet chocolate coating
4 cups rice cereal
1 8-ounce package pitted dates, chopped
1 cup chopped nuts

In a large saucepan melt butter over low heat. Add marshmallows and milk. Heat until melted, stirring constantly. Stir in chocolate until melted. Remove from heat. Cool until thick and heavy. Blend in cereal, dates and nuts. Pat into a rectangle; cut into bars. Keep refrigerated.

Chocolate-Walnut Bars

2 cups semi-sweet chocolate coating
1/4 cup confectioners' sugar
2 tablespoons corn syrup
12 drops concentrated butter-rum flavor
1/2 cup finely chopped walnuts
1/2 cup crushed vanilla wafers
1 teaspoon water
1 egg white

Melt chocolate. Add sugar, corn syrup and flavoring; mix thoroughly. Mixture will be thick. Combine nuts and crushed wafers. Roll chocolate mixture into small logs or balls. Add water to egg white; whip slightly with fork. Dip each ball into egg, then in nut mixture pressing firmly into candy. Candy should be completely coated.

Marbled Bark

1 pound white coating
4 tablespoons paramount crystals OR corn oil, divided
1 pound pink coating
6 drops cherry OR raspberry concentrated flavoring

Melt white coating. Add 2 tablespoons crystals or oil. In separate saucepan melt pink coating. Add remaining crystals or oil and flavoring. Spread pink coating on waxed paper. Dribble white coating over pink coating. With a knife cut through both colors to marblize. Let set up; cut into squares.

Creamy Chocolate Centers

4 tablespoons water
1/4 cup butter
1/2 cup semi-sweet chocolate
3-1/4 cups confectioners' sugar, divided
1/2 teaspoon vanilla
1/2 cup finely chopped walnuts OR pecans

In heavy saucepan combine water, butter and chocolate; heat over low heat until butter and chocolate are melted. Remove from heat. Add 1-1/2 cups confectioners' sugar to hot mixture; beat until smooth. Add 1 more cup confectioners' sugar; beat. Add vanilla and remaining confectioners' sugar, beat until smooth. Add nuts. More confectioners' sugar may be added if mixture is too soft to handle. Mixture will get stiffer as it cools. Makes about 30 centers.

Jiffy Peanut Butter Treats

1/4 cup peanut butter
3 tablespoons sweetened condensed milk
1/4 cup finely chopped blanched peanuts

Mix peanut butter and sweetened condensed milk. Roll into small balls, then roll balls in chopped peanuts. Place on waxed paper and dribble melted coating over. Makes 12 balls. When the chocolate sets up, place each ball in paper candy cup.

Leopard Butter

2 cups white coating, melted
1/2 cup peanut butter
1/2 cup butterscotch coating

Blend white coating and peanut butter. Spread on waxed paper. Spoon various sized spots of butterscotch coating over peanut butter mixture. Let set up; break into pieces.

Hurry Up Peanut Butter Fudge

4 cups real milk chocolate
4 cups white compound chocolate
2 cups peanut butter
1-1/2 cups marshmallow cream
1-1/2 cups chopped, blanched peanuts
1/2 teaspoon salt

Melt chocolates, blend in peanut butter, marshmallow cream, peanuts and salt. Beat smooth and pat into a buttered 11- x 7- x 2-inch pan. Refrigerate until set. Cut into squares. **NOTE:** Chocolate may be used in either wafer form or block form, finely chopped.

Raisin Clusters

1-1/2 cups sweet chocolate coating
1 cup semi-sweet chocolate coating
1/2 cup sweetened condensed milk
1/4 cup marshmallow cream
1/2 teaspoon vanilla
1 cup raisins
1/2 cup nuts

Melt chocolates together over low heat. Add the rest of ingredients. Drop by spoonfuls in clusters on waxed paper. Let cool. Makes 20 clusters.

Potato-Peppermint Fudge

1/2 cup mashed potatoes
2 tablespoons butter
1-3/4 cups chocolate powdered drink mix
1 tablespoon corn syrup
5 drops peppermint oil
1/4 cup toasted wheat germ
3/4 cup finely chopped pecans

Mix all ingredients thoroughly. Pat in buttered 6-inch square pan. Refrigerate several hours. Cut into squares to serve. Keep refrigerated. Makes 16-20 pieces. **NOTE:** A small pan may be formed out of heavy foil.

Nutty Candy Bars

1/2 pound sweet chocolate
1/2 pound semi-sweet chocolate
1/2 cup EACH cashews and pecans

Line shallow candy bar molds with thin layer of melted chocolate. Let set up. Blend chocolates; add nuts. Pat mixture into prepared molds. **NOTE:** If not using molds, mixture may be patted into a rectangle on waxed paper; cut into bars when set up. Dip bars in melted chocolate.

Zebra Butter

3 tablespoons cocoa butter
2 cups white coating, melted
1/2 cup semi-sweet chocolate coating, melted

Add cocoa butter to white coating; stir until dissolved. Partially cool. Spread on waxed paper. Pour chocolate coating in vertical strips over white coating. Run a knife through vertically only. Let set up, break into pieces. (This will take longer to set up than other "butters" because of addition of cocoa butter.)

Mint Rocky Road

2 cups semi-sweet chocolate flavored wafers
3 drops peppermint oil
1-1/2 cups miniature marshmallows
1/2 cup chopped nuts

Melt chocolate. Add peppermint oil. Mix in marshmallows and nuts. Spread on waxed paper and let set up. Store in air tight container. **NOTE:** Marshmallow dries out easily. You may want to cut just before serving.

Delicious Quick Fudge

2-1/2 pounds real chocolate, melted
1 cup whipping cream, heated to 210° F.
1 cup marshmallow cream
1 teaspoon lecithin

Blend ingredients together, just until well mixed. Do not over mix. Pour into a buttered 9 inch square pan.

Easy Apricot Centers

1-1/2 cups ground dry apricots
   (about 11 ounces)
6 tablespoons butter, melted
2 tablespoons orange juice
1 pound confectioners' sugar
White OR chocolate coating

Mix all ingredients together except coating, kneading with your hands to blend. Roll into small balls and dip in coating.

Party Pretties

1 pound white compound coating
1/2 cup butter
1 cup chopped pecans OR walnuts
1 teaspoon vanilla
1 10-1/2-ounce package multicolored
   miniature marshmallows
Confectioners' sugar

Melt white compound, add butter; stir to blend. Add nuts, vanilla and marshmallows; mix well. Form into rolls, using confectioners' sugar to dust. Wrap in plastic wrap and chill. Slice and serve. Makes 40 pieces.

Sweet Treats

1 cup milk chocolate
2 tablespoons butter
1 egg
1 cup confectioners' sugar
1 cup chopped pecans OR walnuts
2 cups miniature marshmallows
Shredded OR flaked coconut, chopped fine

Melt chocolate and butter together. Remove from heat; beat egg into mixture. Stir in sugar, nuts and marshmallows. Let stand a few minutes. Shape into balls. Roll in coconut. Keep refrigerated. Makes about 20 pieces.

Layered Coconut Chews

5 cups coconut dough, divided
Lemon flavoring
Yellow food coloring
Orange flavoring
Orange coloring
Lime flavoring
Green coloring
Raspberry flavoring
Pink food coloring

Divide coconut dough into 5, 1-cup balls. Mix lemon flavoring and yellow food coloring with 1 cup coconut dough. Mix orange flavoring with orange coloring with 1 cup coconut dough. Continue to mix each ball of dough with flavoring and coloring. One cup of dough should be left without coloring or flavoring. Pat each ball into a rectangle on waxed paper. Cover with another piece of waxed paper. Roll thin. Roll each layer the same thickness. Remove top layer of waxed paper from each color of candy, place on layer below. Peel other layer of waxed paper off. A thin layer of melted caramel may be added on the center layer.

Malted Milk Rocks

1/2 cup white coating
1-3/4 cups Malted Milk Crunch
3 tablespoons marshmallow cream
Chocolate coating, melted

Melt coating. Add malted milk and marshmallow cream. Blend together. Press into small balls. Dip in chocolate coating. Makes 40 balls.

Surprises

1 pound butterscotch wafers
1 cup shoestring potatoes
1/4 cup peanut butter
1 cup chopped peanuts

Melt butterscotch coating, using a double boiler or microwave. Remove from heat and add the rest of ingredients. Spread out on wax paper; let set up. Break into bite-size pieces.

Shown on opposite page: Layered Coconut Chews.

Tiger Butter

2 cups white chocolate coating, melted
1/2 cup peanut butter
1 cup sweet chocolate coating, melted

Melt white coating; add peanut butter. Pour out on waxed paper. Melt sweet chocolate. Spoon over the white chocolate mixture, marblize with knife. When set up, cut or break into serving pieces.

Pretzel Bark

1 12-ounce bag pretzels, crushed
1 pound chocolate flavored coating OR white coating

Puncture pretzel bag with knife, then crush pretzels in bag with a rolling pin. Melt coating. Add pretzels and spread on waxed paper to set up. Break into serving size pieces.

After Dinner Cinnamon Creams

1-1/2 cups sugar
Pinch salt
1/2 cup whipping cream
1/4 cup milk
1 tablespoon butter
6 drops cinnamon oil
Red food coloring

In a 2-quart saucepan combine all ingredients except flavoring and coloring; cover. Cook until steam comes from under lid. Remove lid, insert thermometer. Cook to 240° without stirring. Pour on cold surface. When comfortably warm, work with fondant spatula. When creamy, let candy rest. Knead until smooth. Form into balls; flatten with fork.

Crunchy Nibbles

Thinly sliced white OR wheat bread
Butter, melted
Milk chocolate, melted

Remove crusts from bread. With pastry brush generously spread both sides with melted butter. Cut each slice into bite size pieces. Place in a 15- x 11- x 1-inch pan. Toast in a 300° oven with crisp and golden brown. Cool completely. Dip pieces of toast in melted milk chocolate.

Chocolate Nut Logs

1 cup light brown sugar
3/4 cup granulated sugar
1/2 cup maple syrup
1 cup half and half cream
3 tablespoons butter
Pinch salt
1 cup semi-sweet chocolate wafers
1 teaspoon vanilla
1 egg white
1 cup finely chopped pecans

In a heavy 3-quart saucepan combine sugars, syrup, cream, butter, salt and chocolate. Place over moderate heat. Stir until mixture starts to boil. Continue cooking to 236°. Stir occasionally. Cool to 110°. Beat until it holds shape. Add vanilla while beating. Turn out on buttered surface. Knead until smooth. Form candy into three rolls. Brush each with egg white. Roll in finely chopped nuts; press nuts firmly into candy. Wrap rolls in plastic film, then in foil. Slice as needed.

Krispy Date Candy

1/2 cup non-fat dry milk
1/2 cup butter
1/2 cup sugar
1 tablespoon corn syrup
8 ounces chopped dates
1 egg, beaten
3 cups rice cereal
1 cup chopped walnuts

Cream milk and butter. Add sugar and corn syrup. Blend in dates. Transfer to a heavy 2-quart saucepan. Put egg in mixing bowl; beat. Set aside. Cook date mixture on top of stove several minutes, until mixture comes to full rolling boil. Stir constantly. Remove from stove. Add beaten egg, return to stove. Cook 2 minutes on stove. Stir after each 30 seconds. Mixture should again come to full, rolling boil. Remove from heat. Combine cereal and nuts in bowl. Pour hot candy over mixture, stir thoroughly. Pat into a 11- x 7- x 2-inch buttered pan. Let cool. Cut into squares when cool.

Shown on opposite page: Tiger Butter, Zebra Butter, Health Candy, Chocolate Walnut Bars, Karin's Apriconut Balls.

Caramel Almond Squares

1-1/2 pounds white chocolate, divided
1 cup marshmallow cream
1 cup chopped almonds, toasted
1 pound caramel
1/4 cup toasted coconut OR rice cereal

Melt 1 pound white chocolate. Add marshmallow cream and almonds; blend well. Pat into a 13- x 9- x 2-inch pan. Melt caramel. Pour evenly over white chocolate layer. Mix 1/2 pound melted white chocolate and coconut. Spread over caramel layer; cool. Cut into squares with sharp knife.

Spicy Mexican Balls

2 cups sugar
1 cup water
9 egg yolks, beaten
4 ounces blanched almonds, ground fine
1/2 teaspoon cinnamon
1/4 teaspoon cloves
1/4 cup confectioners' sugar

Boil sugar and water to 275° or until syrup spins a long thread. Pour hot syrup slowly into beating egg yolks. Add almonds and spices and return mixture to a heavy 2-quart pan. Cook on low heat for 10 minutes or until mixture is very thick. Stir constantly. Remove from heat. Stir until firm and cool. Spread confectioners' sugar on tray. Spoon mixture on sugar. Form into small balls, roll in confectioners' sugar.

Pecan Clusters

2-1/2 cups granulated sugar
4 tablespoons butter
1/8 teaspoon salt
1/2 cup evaporated milk
3/4 pound sweet chocolate coating, melted
1 cup marshmallow cream
2 cups chopped pecans
1 teaspoon vanilla

In a heavy 3-quart saucepan cook sugar, butter, salt and milk. Stir constantly. Add the rest of ingredients. Blend well; drop by spoonfuls on waxed paper.

Top of the Stove Date Cookies

1 8-ounce package pitted dates
1/2 cup flaked coconut
1/2 cup granulated sugar
1/4 cup butter
1 beaten egg
1/8 teaspoon salt
1-1/2 cups rice cereal
1/2 cup walnuts
1 teaspoon vanilla

In a heavy 2-quart saucepan combine dates, coconut, sugar, butter, egg and salt. Cook over medium heat. Stir constantly until thick. Remove from heat. Add the rest of ingredients. Let cool. Shape into 1-inch balls, roll in granulated sugar.

Cut-Out Mints

1-1/2 tablespoons butter
1 tablespoon shortening
Pinch salt
1-1/4 teaspoons tepid water
4 drops peppermint oil
Food coloring
2 to 2-1/2 cups confectioners' sugar

Combine butter, shortening, salt, water, flavoring, coloring and 1 cup confectioners' sugar. Beat until smooth. Add 1 additional cup sugar; beat. Turn out and knead. Add more sugar if necessary. Roll out in rectangle and cut with tiny aspic cutters. Gather up scraps and form in a roll. Slice into small round mints. Let dry to form crust on each side. Store in air-tight container.

Raspberry Candy Creams

1/3 cup granulated sugar
1/3 cup light brown sugar
1/3 cup corn syrup
1/4 cup water
1 tablespoon PLUS 1 teaspoon dry egg whites
3 tablespoons water
1/3 teaspoon vanilla
1 tablespoon raspberry jam
2 tablespoons melted pink coating

In a saucepan combine sugars, corn syrup and water; cover. Bring to boil. Remove lid, insert thermometer. Cook to 240° without stirring. Meanwhile soak egg whites in 3 tablespoons water. Stir to moisten. When thermometer reads 240°, remove from heat. Pour in a thin stream into egg whites while beating. Beat until mixture is thick and fluffy. Stir in vanilla, raspberry jam and pink coating. Line candy mold with melted chocolate. Let set up. Fill pastry bag with raspberry mixture and fill chocolate molds. Cover with melted chocolate; let set up.

Krispy Caramel Bars

5-1/2 cups rice cereal
2 tablespoons butter
1/4 cup PLUS 2 tablespoons peanut butter
2-1/2 cups miniature marshmallows
1/2 teaspoon vanilla
1/2 pound caramel
1/2 pound light chocolate flavored coating
1 tablespoon paramount crystals OR corn oil

Measure rice cereal into large buttered bowl; set aside. In a double boiler or heavy saucepan combine butter, peanut butter and marshmallows over low heat until smooth and thick. Add vanilla; beat. Pour over rice cereal. Mix together with spoon and then with hands. Pat into buttered 9-inch square pan. Melt caramel over low heat; spread evenly over cereal mixture. Let cool. Melt chocolate and paramount crystals. Spread over cooled caramel. Let chocolate set; cut into bars.

Chocolate Pralines

1-1/2 cups granulated sugar
1 cup light brown sugar
1/2 cup whole milk
2 tablespoons whipping cream
1/8 teaspoon salt
1 cup semi-sweet chocolate wafers
2 cups coarsely chopped pecans
2 tablespoons butter
1 teaspoon vanilla

In a heavy 3-quart saucepan combine sugars, milk, cream, salt and chocolate wafers. Place over medium heat. Stir occasionally until chocolate melts and sugars dissolve. Turn heat higher and continue cooking, without stirring to 230°. Add nuts and butter; cook to 235°, stir constantly. Remove candy from heat; stir in vanilla. Beat with wooden spoon only until candy starts to thicken. Drop from spoon onto waxed paper.

Black Walnut Nuggets

1/2 pound dry fondant
10 drops invertase, optional
3 tablespoons water
1/8 teaspoon butter flavoring
1/4 teaspoon vanilla
Pinch salt
1 tablespoon dry egg white
1 tablespoon corn syrup
1 tablespoon invert sugar*
1/2 pound dry fondant
3-1/2 tablespoons butter
1/4 cup finely chopped black walnuts
Chocolate coating
1/2 cup finely chopped black walnuts

*Recipe for invert sugar is on page 52. In a mixing bowl place 1/2 pound dry fondant, invertase, water, butter flavoring, vanilla, salt, egg white, corn syrup and invert sugar. Mix on slow speed until blended. Whip on high for 3 minutes. Add other 1/2 pound fondant, butter and 1/4 cup walnuts. Mix slowly to blend completely. Mixture should be quite firm. More water or fondant may be added to get easy-to-handle consistency. Roll into balls. Add 1/2 cup walnuts to chocolate coating. Dip balls in chocolate-walnut mixture.

Chewy Coconut Bars

1-1/2 cups corn syrup
1/8 teaspoon salt
1/2 cup water
1 cup sugar
3 cups desiccated OR macaroon coconut
1/2 cup candied cherries AND pineapple
1/2 cup raisins
1/2 cup chopped pecans
Semi-sweet chocolate, melted

In small saucepan combine corn syrup, salt, water and sugar. Cover tightly. Cook until steam comes from under lid. Remove lid and insert thermometer. Cook to 236°. Meanwhile place coconut, candied fruit, raisins and pecans in large buttered bowl; mix well. Pour cooked syrup over fruit and nuts. Mix thoroughly. Pour out on buttered marble slab or buttered cookie sheet. Pack into a 3/8-inch rectangular shape. Cool, cut into bars. Spread apart, let dry. Dip in semi-sweet chocolate.

Coconut Clusters

2 cups brown sugar
1 cup white sugar
1-1/4 cups half and half cream
2 tablespoons butter
1 teaspoon vanilla
1/2 teaspoon coconut flavoring
1-3/4 cups shredded coconut

In a 3-quart saucepan mix sugars, cream and butter. Cook to 238°. Stir until sugar is dissolved. Remove from heat, cool 40 minutes. Add flavorings. Beat until mixture thickens and gets creamy. Blend in coconut. Drop by spoonsful on wax paper.

Sea Foam

1-3/4 cups light brown sugar
3/4 cup granulated sugar
1/2 cup hot water
1/4 cup corn syrup
1/4 teaspoon salt
2 egg whites
1 teaspoon vanilla
1/2 cup small pecan pieces

In a heavy 2-quart saucepan combine sugars, water, corn syrup and salt. Cook covered, until steam comes from under lid. Remove lid, continue cooking without stirring. When mixture reaches 250°, beat egg whites in a bowl. Continue cooking syrup to 260°. Pour hot syrup in thin stream over beaten egg whites. Add vanilla. Continue beating until mixture loses gloss and stands in soft peaks. Add nuts. Drop in mounds on waxed paper.

Chewy Chocolate Toffee

2 cups granulated sugar
1/4 cup cocoa
1 cup dark corn syrup
1/4 teaspoon salt
1/2 cup whipping cream
1/4 cup butter

In a 4-quart saucepan, mix all ingredients. Stir frequently until boiling starts. Stir occasionally. Lower heat as candy thickens. Line an 8-inch square pan with foil; butter generously. Cook toffee to 250°. Pour in prepared pan, let cool and set up. Cut into small, narrow rectangles. Wrap in clear plastic film.

Almond Butter Logs

3-1/2 cups granulated sugar
1/2 cup brown sugar
2 tablespoons corn syrup
1/2 cup whipping cream
1 cup evaporated milk
1/2 cup butter
1/8 teaspoon salt
1 teaspoon vanilla
3/4 cup marshmallow cream
2 cups sliced, chopped, roasted almonds
Sweet chocolate, melted

In a 3-quart saucepan combine sugars, corn syrup, cream, milk, butter and salt. Cook over medium-high heat. Bring to full rolling boil. Continue cooking to 238°, stirring frequently. Pour on marble slab or other cold surface. Let cool until warm. Work this candy warmer than most fondants. Work with fondant paddle until mixture gets creamy. Add vanilla. Work in marshmallow cream and almonds. Mound up; let cool. Form into small logs. Dip in sweet chocolate or wrap securely and refrigerate until ready to use.

Invert Sugar

8 cups granulated sugar
3 cups hot water
1-1/2 teaspoons citric acid crystals OR juice of
    two lemons

In a heavy 4-quart saucepan, combine all ingredients. Bring to boil. Stir constantly to dissolve sugar. Lower heat; simmer for 30 minutes. Stir occasionally. Makes 3 pints. Store in a tight container on the shelf. **NOTE:** Lemons may change flavor of candy.

Honey Mints

1 tablespoon honey
2 teaspoons butter
1/4 cup non-fat dry milk
Pinch salt
2 teaspoons hot water
2 drops peppermint oil
1 to 1-1/2 cups confectioners' sugar

Combine honey, butter, dry milk, salt, water and peppermint oil in mixing bowl; beat smooth. Add 1 cup sugar; beat smooth. Turn out and knead, adding more sugar to form pie dough consistency. Form into rolls and slice or pat into rectangle. Cut into small shapes. Makes 30 to 40 mints.

Marshmallows

1/4 cup unflavored gelatin
1/2 cup cold water
1/2 cup hot water
2-1/2 cups granulated sugar
1-1/2 cups invert sugar*
3/4 cup light corn syrup
1 teaspoon vanilla

*Recipe for invert sugar is on page 52. In mixing bowl soak gelatin in cold water. In saucepan combine hot water, sugar and invert sugar. Heat to 210° or just to boiling point. Pour hot mixture over gelatin. Blend on low speed of mixer for 30 seconds. Beat on high speed for 1 minute. Add corn syrup and vanilla as mixture beats. Continue beating until marshmallow is white, doubled in bulk and stands in soft peaks. Pour into a buttered 15- x 12- x 1-inch pan. Let set 24 hours before cutting into squares. Marshmallow squares may be dipped in chocolate.

VARIATIONS:

Coconut-Marshmallow Squares: Place marshmallow squares in colander. Pour COLD water over and roll each square in toasted coconut.

Rocky Road: Cut marshmallow in small pieces. Combine with toasted nuts, small squares of caramel and melted chocolate. Spread in a buttered pan. Let set.

Marshmallow Cream

2-1/4 cups invert sugar*
4-1/2 tablespoons dried egg whites
2-1/4 cups corn syrup
1 teaspoon vanilla

*Recipe for invert sugar is on page 52. In mixer bowl combine 1-1/8 cups invert sugar with egg white. Blend on low speed. In saucepan combine remaining invert sugar with corn syrup. Heat to 210° or just to boiling point. Add hot syrup to egg white mixture, beating constantly. Add vanilla. Continue beating until mixture becomes white, fluffy and doubles in bulk. Makes about 3-1/2 quarts. Marshmallow cream does not need to be refrigerated. Will keep for several months. If mixture should separate, mix together before using.

Shown on opposite page: Layered Coconut Chews, Dipped Marshmallow, Coconut Marshmallow, Peanut Butter Caramel Bars.

Candied Violets

Fresh violets
4 tablespoons water
2 tablespoons gum arabic
1/2 cup sugar
4 tablespoons water
1 tablespoon corn syrup

Pick violets; trim off all of stem. Lay violets on waxed paper. Bring 4 tablespoons water to boil. Add gum arabic. Remove from heat. Stir to dissolve. Let cool. Using a small, good quality brush, paint violets on one side with gum solution. Let dry. Turn over; paint other side. When violets dry, bring sugar, water and corn syrup to boil in small saucepan. Cover tightly. Remove lid when steam appears. Cook to 238°. Let cool. Carefully dip each violet into syrup and let dry on waxed paper.

Coconut Squares

1/3 cup light corn syrup
2 tablespoons sugar
2 tablespoons water
2-1/4 cups flaked coconut
1 teaspoon vanilla
1/2 cup semi-sweet chocolate wafers
1/2 cup butterscotch wafers
2 teaspoons paramount crystals OR 1 teaspoon corn oil
1/3 cup slivered almonds

In a small saucepan with tight lid cook corn syrup, sugar and water until steam comes from under lid. Remove lid; insert thermometer. Cook to 234°. Add coconut and vanilla; blend well. Pat candy into buttered 8-inch square pan. While candy cools, melt semi-sweet chocolate and butterscotch wafers. Blend paramount crystals into chocolate mixture. Mix well. Spread chocolate mixture over cooled candy. Sprinkle almonds on chocolate. Let set up. Cut into small squares.

Peanut Butter Centers

1/2 cup butter
1-1/2 cups peanut butter
1/4 cup corn syrup
3/4 to 1 pound confectioners' sugar
Semi-sweet chocolate, melted

Combine ingredients except chocolate coating. Roll into balls and dip in melted chocolate.

Pecan Divinity

2-1/2 cups granulated sugar
1/2 cup light corn syrup
1/2 cup water
1/4 teaspoon salt
2 egg whites
1 teaspoon vanilla
2/3 cup finely chopped pecans

In a 2-quart saucepan cook sugar, corn syrup, water and salt. Cover tightly. Remove lid and insert thermometer. When syrup gets to 240° start beating egg whites. Cook syrup to 248°. Pour half of hot syrup over beating eggs. Cook the rest of syrup to 272°. Keep egg white and syrup mixture beating while adding the rest of syrup. Add vanilla. Beat until mixture is thick, fluffy and starts to lose gloss and holds soft peaks. Fold in nuts. Drop from teaspoon into small mounds on waxed paper.

VARIATION:

Chocolate Pecan Divinity: Prepare as for pecan divinity. Fold in melted semi-sweet chocolate pieces to batter when folding in nuts.

Three Layer Squares

1/2 cup butter
1/4 cup semi-sweet chocolate coating
1 egg
1-1/4 cups sugar
2 cups crushed graham crackers
1 teaspoon vanilla
1 cup desiccated coconut
1/2 cup nuts
1/4 cup butter
2 tablespoons whipping cream
2 cups confectioners' sugar
1 teaspoon vanilla
1-1/2 cups semi-sweet chocolate coating
1-1/2 tablespoons paramount crystals OR corn oil

Melt butter and 1/4 cup chocolate. Blend in egg; beat well. Add sugar, crumbs, vanilla, coconut and nuts; mix well. Press into ungreased 11- x 7- x 2-inch pan. Mix 1/4 cup butter, cream, confectioners' sugar and vanilla. Beat well. Spread over crumb mixture. Melt 1-1/2 cups chocolate. Add paramount crystals or corn oil. Spread over white filling. Chill. Cut into 1-inch squares. Store in refrigerator.

Shown on opposite page: Hazelnut Nougat, Peanut Butter Nougat Candy Bar Filling, Black Walnut Nugget, Peanut Butter Caramel Bars, Chocolate Butter Mints.

Almond Nougat

1 cup invert sugar*, divided
2-1/2 tablespoons dried egg whites
1 cup corn syrup
1/2 cup brown sugar
1/2 teaspoon vanilla
1/3 cup white chocolate compound
1/8 teaspoon almond flavoring
Sweet OR semi-sweet chocolate, melted

*Recipe for invert sugar is on page 52. In a large mixing bowl combine 1/2 cup invert sugar and egg whites. In a small saucepan bring corn syrup, brown sugar and remaining invert sugar to boil. Stir only until boiling starts. continue cooking without stirring to 230°. Pour hot syrup in thin stream into beating egg white mixture. Mix on low speed to blend. Whip on high speed until light and fluffy. Add vanilla while beating. Cool completely. Add white chocolate compound and almond flavoring to cup of nougat. Stir just to blend. Store remaining nougat mixture in a covered container. Line candy bar molds with melted chocolate. Pat filling into prepared mold. Seal with more chocolate. Chill for 5 minutes. Remove from mold. Makes 8 candy bars.

Light Chocolate Nougat

1 cup invert sugar*, divided
2-1/2 tablespoons dried egg whites
1 cup corn syrup
1/2 cup brown sugar
1/2 teaspoon vanilla
1/3 cup real milk chocolate wafers, melted
Sweet OR semi-sweet chocolate, melted

*Recipe for invert sugar is on page 52. In a large mixing bowl combine 1/2 cup invert sugar and egg whites. In a small saucepan bring to boil corn syrup, brown sugar and remaining invert sugar. Stir only until boiling starts. continue cooking without stirring to 230°. Pour hot syrup in thin stream into beating egg white mixture. Mix on low speed to blend. Whip on high speed until light and fluffy. Add vanilla while beating. Cool completely. Add 1/3 cup melted chocolate wafers to 1 cup nougat mixture. Stir just to blend. Store remaining nougat mixture in a covered container. Line candy bar molds with melted chocolate. Pat filling into prepared mold. Seal with more chocolate. Chill for 5 minutes. Remove from mold. Makes 8 candy bars.

Unbaked Cookies

2 tablespoons cocoa
2 cups granulated sugar
1/2 cup milk
1/4 cup butter
3 cups quick oats
1/2 cup peanut butter
1/2 teaspoon vanilla
Coconut, optional
Nuts, optional

In a 2-quart saucepan combine cocoa, sugar, milk and butter. Bring to boil for one minute. Remove from heat. Add the rest of ingredients. While mixture is warm, drop by tablespoons on waxed paper.

Raspberry Jellies

2 boxes Sure-Jel
1-1/2 cups water
1/2 teaspoon baking soda
1 cup granulated sugar OR confectioners' sugar
1 12-ounce jar raspberry jam
1-1/2 cups corn syrup
1 /2 teaspoon citric acid
1 teaspoon water
Granulated sugar
Chocolate coating, optional

In a 1-quart saucepan mix Sure-Jel, 1-1/2 cups water and baking soda. Place over medium heat; stir until mixture is hot and foaming stops. Do not boil. In a 4-quart saucepan mix sugar, jam and corn syrup. Place over high heat. Bring to boil. Add hot Sure-Jel mixture and continue cooking to 225°. Stir constantly. Remove from heat. Combine citric acid and water. Add 1 teaspoon solution. Pour into a buttered 8-inch square pan. Let set up. Cut into small squares; roll in sugar. Candy may also be dipped in melted chocolate, if desired.

Homemade Sweetened Condensed Milk

1 cup non-fat dry milk
2/3 cup granulated sugar
1/3 cup boiling water
1/4 cup butter, melted

Combine ingredients in blender. Blend until smooth. Scrape down sides occasionally. Refrigerate in covered container.

Hazel Nut Nougat

1 cup invert sugar*, divided
2-1/2 tablespoons dried egg whites
1 cup corn syrup
1/2 cup brown sugar
1/2 teaspoon vanilla
1/4 cup filbert paste
1/2 pound sweet OR semi-sweet chocolate,
  melted
1/3 cup filbert paste

*Recipe for invert sugar is on page 52. In a large mixing bowl combine 1/2 cup invert sugar and egg whites. In a small saucepan bring corn syrup, brown sugar and remaining invert sugar to boil. Stir only until boiling starts. Continue cooking without stirring to 230°. Pour hot syrup in thin stream into beating egg white mixture. Mix on low speed to blend. Whip on high speed until light and fluffy. Add vanilla while beating. Cool completely. Add 1/4 cup filbert paste to 1 cup nougat mixture. Stir just to blend. Store remaining nougat mixture in a covered container. Blend melted chocolate and 1/3 cup filbert paste. Line candy bar molds with melted chocolate. Pat filling into prepared mold. Seal with more chocolate. Chill for 5 minutes. Remove from mold. Makes 8 candy bars.

Rich Chocolate Nougat

1 cup invert sugar*, divided
2-1/2 tablespoons dried egg whites
1 cup corn syrup
1/2 cup brown sugar
1/2 teaspoon vanilla
1/3 cup semi-sweet chocolate, melted
Semi-sweet chocolate, melted

*Recipe for invert sugar is on page 52. In a large mixing bowl combine 1/2 cup invert sugar and egg whites. In a small saucepan bring to boil corn syrup, brown sugar and remaining invert sugar. Stir only until boiling starts. continue cooking without stirring to 230°. Pour hot syrup in thin stream into beating egg white mixture. Mix on low speed to blend. Whip on high speed until light and fluffy. Add vanilla while beating. Cool completely. Add 1/3 cup semi-sweet chocolate to 1 cup nougat mixture. Stir just to blend. Store remaining nougat mixture in a covered container. Line candy bar molds with melted chocolate. Pat filling into prepared mold. Seal with more chocolate. Chill for 5 minutes. Remove from mold. Makes 8 candy bars.

Chocolate Covered Cherries With Stems

Maraschino cherries
3 cups dry fondant
1/2 cup water OR cherry juice
6 drops invertase, optional
Chocolate compound for dipping

Drain cherries on paper toweling. Mix fondant with water or cherry juice. Heat in double boiler until melted. Hot water may be added if fondant is too thick. Dip each cherry in fondant enough to cover stem slightly. Let fondant set up. Dip as many times as desired. Let fondant cool completely. Dip in compound chocolate. Chocolate should cover all fondant.

Peanut Candy

2 cups granulated sugar
1/2 teaspoon cream of tartar
1 cup water
12 ounces salted, blanched peanuts, finely
  chopped
1 teaspoon vanilla

In a small saucepan mix sugar, cream of tartar and water. Cover tightly. Cook until steam comes from under lid. Remove lid; insert thermometer. Cook to 236°. Add chopped peanuts; remove from heat. Beat until mixture thickens and becomes sugary. Add vanilla while beating. Pour in buttered 13- x 9- x 2-inch pan. Cut into squares while slightly warm.

Peanut Patties

2 cups sugar
1 cup brown sugar
1/2 cup butter
3-1/2 cups light corn syrup
2 teaspoons salt (less if peanuts are salted)
1/2 cup water
1/4 teaspoon baking soda
5 cups blanched peanuts, chopped

In a 3-quart saucepan combine sugars, butter, corn syrup, salt and water. Cover tightly. Bring to boil; uncover. Insert thermometer. Cook, without stirring to 244°. Remove from heat; stir in soda. Add nuts and mix well. Drop from spoon into well buttered muffin tins or well buttered cookie sheet. Let cool. Wrap in clear plastic wrap.

Peanut Butter Caramel Bars

3 tablespoons dry egg whites
2 tablespoons water
1/4 cup invert sugar*
2 cups granulated sugar
1/3 cup water
2/3 cup invert sugar*
1 cup corn syrup
1/4 teaspoon salt
1 teaspoon vanilla
2 tablespoons vegetable shortening
1/2 cup peanut butter
1 pound caramel
2 cups blanched, roasted, chopped peanuts

*Recipe for invert sugar is on page 52. Blend egg whites with 2 tablespoons water in bowl; beat until soft peaks form. Gradually add 1/4 cup invert sugar. Whip until mixture is light and fluffy. In 2-quart saucepan, combine granulated sugar, 1/3 cup water, 2/3 cup invert sugar, corn syrup and salt. Cover and cook until steam comes from under lid. Remove lid and insert thermometer. Cook to 250°. Pour 1-1/3 cups boiling syrup over egg white mixture. Continue cooking remainder of syrup until it reaches 280°. While cooking, continue to beat eggs. Pour syrup over eggs and beat until soft peaks form. Blend in vanilla, shortening and peanut butter. Pour into a buttered 13- x 9- x 2-inch pan. Melt caramel. Sprinkle chopped peanuts over candy in pan. Pour melted caramel evenly over peanuts. Let set overnight. Cut into small bars or dip in melted chocolate. Wrap in plastic wrap.

Coconut Bonbons

1 cup sugar
1-3/4 cups corn syrup
2 tablespoons invert sugar*
1/2 cup water
1/4 teaspoon salt
4-1/4 cups dessicated coconut
1 teaspoon almond flavoring
1 teaspoon vanilla
Colored coating, optional
Fondant, optional

*Recipe for invert sugar is on page 52. In a 2-quart saucepan cook sugar, corn syrup, invert sugar, water and salt until steam comes from under lid. Remove lid, insert thermometer. Cook to 234°. Remove from heat. Add coconut and flavorings. Let cool. Form into balls and dip in colored coating or melted fondant.

Chocolate Candy Bar

1/3 cup granulated sugar
1/3 cup light brown sugar
1/3 cup corn syrup
1/4 cup water
1 tablespoon PLUS 1 teaspoon dry egg whites
3 tablespoons water
1/3 teaspoon vanilla
3 tablespoons semi-sweet chocolate, melted
Dipping chocolate

In a saucepan combine sugars, corn syrup and water; cover. Bring to boil. Remove lid, insert thermometer. Cook to 240° without stirring. Meanwhile soak egg whites in 3 tablespoons water. Stir to moisten. When thermometer reads 230°, start beating egg white mixture. When syrup reaches 240°, remove from heat. Pour in a thin stream into egg whites while beating. Beat until mixture is thick and fluffy. Stir in vanilla and melted chocolate. Roll into balls and dip in chocolate.

Peanut Butter Marshmallow Eggs

1-1/2 cups butter, softened
5 to 6 cups confectioners' sugar, divided
1 cup peanut butter
1-3/4 cups marshmallow cream
2 teaspoons vanilla
Chocolate for dipping

Cream butter and 2 cups confectioners' sugar in mixing bowl until light and fluffy. Add peanut butter, marshmallow cream and vanilla; blend well. Gradually add remaining confectioners' sugar. Add enough to make an easily molded consistency. Form into egg shapes, dip in chocolate.

Filbert Fudge

1/2 pound sweet chocolate
2/3 cup filbert paste, divided
1/2 pound semi-sweet chocolate

Melt sweet chocolate. Blend in 1/3 cup filbert paste. Spread mixture on waxed paper. While mixture is setting up, melt semi-sweet chocolate. Add remaining filbert paste. Spread over first mixture on waxed paper. Cut layered fudge into squares when firm. **NOTE:** If real chocolate is used, cool to 90° before mixing with filbert paste.

Pecan Rolls

Nougat:
3 tablespoons dry egg whites
2 tablespoons water
1/4 cup invert sugar*
2 cups granulated sugar
1/3 cup water
2/3 cup invert sugar*
1 cup corn syrup
1/4 teaspoon salt
1 teaspoon vanilla
2 tablespoons vegetable shortening

Caramel Coating:
1-1/2 cups granulated sugar
1 cup corn syrup
1 cup sweetened condensed milk
3/4 cup vegetable shortening
1-1/2 cups whipping cream
2 cups chopped pecans

*Recipe for invert sugar is on page 52. **Nougat:** Blend egg whites with 2 tablespoons water in bowl; beat until soft peaks form. Gradually add 1/4 cup invert sugar. Whip until mixture is light and fluffy. Combine granulated sugar, 1/3 cup water, 2/3 cup invert sugar, corn syrup and salt in 2-quart saucepan. Cover and cook until steam comes from under lid. Remove lid and insert thermometer. Cook to 250°. Pour 1-1/3 cups boiling syrup over egg white mixture. Continue cooking remainder of syrup until it reaches 280°. While cooking, continue to beat eggs. Pour syrup over eggs and beat until soft peaks form. Blend in vanilla and shortening. pour into a buttered 13- x 9- x 2-inch pan. Let set up. **Caramel Coating:** Combine all ingredients in a heavy 3-quart saucepan; cook to 242° stirring constantly. Cut nougat into bars and dip in hot caramel coating. Roll in chopped pecans.

Caramelized Chocolate

1 pound white chocolate compound
1 14-ounce can sweetened condensed milk
1 cup chopped pecans

Cook chocolate over boiling water. Stir constantly, until chocolate turns light tan and is quite thick. DO NOT LET IT BURN. When well caramelized, add sweetened condensed milk and nuts. Quickly blend together. Pour out on buttered cookie sheet or on waxed paper. Let set up. When cool cut into squares. Dip in chocolate.

Fudge Rocky Road Drops

1-1/3 cups semi-sweet chocolate wafers
2/3 cup sweetened condensed milk
2 cups miniature marshmallows, divided
1/4 cup crunchy peanut butter
1 teaspoon vanilla
1/2 cup finely chopped peanuts

In double boiler melt chocolate. Blend in sweetened condensed milk. Add 1 cup marshmallows. Stir until melted. Add peanut butter, vanilla and chopped peanuts; blend well. Remove from heat. Let candy cool 8 minutes. Add 1 cup marshmallows. Blend only enough to coat. Marshmallows will melt a little, not completely. Spoon into paper candy cups.

Chewy Almond Toffees

3/4 cup thinly sliced almonds
1-1/3 cups granulated sugar
1/2 cup light corn syrup
1/2 cup dark corn syrup
1/4 teaspoon salt
1/2 cup butter
1 cup half and half cream

Keep almonds warm in 250° oven. In a heavy 3-quart saucepan combine sugar, syrups, salt, butter and cream. Cook to 250°, stirring occasionally. Remove from heat. Add hot almonds; stir. Drop by teaspoons on well buttered cookie sheet or marble slab. When cool, wrap in clear plastic film.

Spiced Nuts

1 12-ounce can deluxe mixed nuts
1 cup pecans
1 cup peanuts
1 egg white
1 teaspoon water
3/4 cup sugar
1 tablespoon pumpkin pie spice

Combine all nuts in medium-sized bowl. In a small bowl mix egg white and water with fork. Add sugar and spice. Pour sugar mixture over nuts. Stir gently until all nuts are coated. Spread on two buttered cookie sheets, making a single layer of nuts. Bake in 300° oven for 20 to 25 minutes or until coating is light brown and crisp. While hot, loosen from bottom of cookie sheets with spatula. Let cool and store in a tight container.

Chocolate-Coconut Balls

1 cup semi-sweet chocolate
1/4 cup butter
1/2 cup sweetened condensed milk
3/4 cup sugar
1 tablespoon corn syrup
1/4 cup water
1 teaspoon vanilla
2 cups finely chopped coconut
1 cup chopped nuts, optional
Confectioners' sugar

In double boiler melt chocolate and butter. Add sweetened condensed milk; blend in. Set aside. In a 1-quart saucepan cook sugar, corn syrup and water until steam comes from under lid. Remove lid, insert thermometer. Cook to 250°. Remove from heat. Stir chocolate mixture into hot syrup. Blend in vanilla, coconut and nuts. Chill in refrigerator until mixture sets up enough to roll into balls. Roll each ball in confectioners' sugar.

Cinnamon Walnuts

1-1/2 cups granulated sugar
1/4 cup evaporated milk
1/4 cup whipping cream
1 tablespoon water
1/4 teaspoon salt
1-1/2 cups walnuts
10 drops cinnamon oil
Semi-sweet chocolate, melted

In a 2-quart saucepan cook sugar, milk, cream, water and salt until it reaches 238°. Stir occasionally. Lower heat as mixture thickens. Remove from heat, stir in walnuts and cinnamon oil. Stir until mixture becomes creamy. Drop small clusters on waxed paper or spread out on waxed paper. Spread apart with forks. When clusters set up, place very closely together and dribble semi-sweet chocolate over them.

Chocolate Covered Cherries

Clear plastic bon bon mold
Compound chocolate for coating molds
3 cups dry fondant
80 to 90 maraschino cherries
Liquid from cherries

Line mold cavities with melted chocolate; set aside. Place dry fondant on tray. Roll cherries in dry fondant. Spread coated cherries on paper towel-lined cookie sheet. Moisten fondant coating with maraschino cherry juice. Roll in fondant. Remove and moisten again with juice. Continue moistening and rolling cherries until they are the size to fit lined molds. Place coated cherries in lined molds. Seal with melted chocolate. Chill in freezer for 5 minutes. When set up, pop out of mold and place in paper candy cups.

Filbert Candy Bars

1/3 cup granulated sugar
1/3 cup light brown sugar
1/3 cup corn syrup
1/4 cup water
1 tablespoon PLUS 1 teaspoon dry egg whites
3 tablespoons water
1/3 teaspoon vanilla
2 tablespoons filbert paste
Dipping chocolate, melted

In a saucepan combine sugars, corn syrup and water; cover. Bring to boil. Remove lid, insert thermometer. Cook to 240° without stirring. Meanwhile soak egg whites in 3 tablespoons water. Stir to moisten. When thermometer reads 230°, start beating egg white mixture. When syrup reaches 240°, remove from heat. Pour syrup in a thin stream into egg whites while beating. Beat until mixture is thick and fluffy. Stir in vanilla and filbert paste. Roll into balls and dip in chocolate.

Citric Jellies

2 cups granulated sugar
1/2 cup water
3-1/2 tablespoons unflavored gelatin
1/4 cup cold water
1/2 cup orange juice
1/4 cup lemon juice
Orange food coloring
Confectioners' sugar

In a 1-quart saucepan cook sugar and 1/2 cup water until steam comes from under lid. Remove lid, insert thermometer. Cook to 255° without stirring. Soften gelatin in 1/4 cup cold water. Add gelatin to cooked syrup. Blend in juices and coloring. Stir to dissolve softened gelatin. Pour into a buttered 8-inch square pan. Let stand until firm. Turn out, cut into squares and roll in confectioners' sugar.

Peanut Butter Candy Bars

1/3 cup granulated sugar
1/2 cup light brown sugar
1/3 cup corn syrup
1/4 cup water
1 tablespoon PLUS 1 teaspoon dry egg whites
3 tablespoons water
1/3 teaspoon vanilla
2 tablespoons peanut butter
Dipping chocolate, melted

In a saucepan combine sugars, corn syrup and water; cover. Bring to boil. Remove lid, insert thermometer. Cook to 240° without stirring. Meanwhile soak egg whites in 3 tablespoons water. Stir to moisten. When thermometer reads 230°, start beating egg white mixture. When syrup reaches 240°, remove from heat. Pour syrup in a thin stream into egg whites while beating. Beat until mixture is thick and fluffy. Stir in vanilla and peanut butter. Roll into balls and dip in chocolate.

Date Logs

3 cups sugar
1 cup milk
1 8-ounce package pitted dates, chopped
1/4 teaspoon salt
1 tablespoon butter
4 cups English walnuts, coarsely chopped

In a heavy 3-quart saucepan combine all ingredients except nuts. Cook mixture to 240°; stirring frequently. As mixture thickens, stir constantly. Remove from heat when mixture reaches 240°. Let cool 30 minutes in pan. Beat for 2 minutes. Blend in nuts. Form into 2 logs on wet towel. Wrap each roll tightly. After 30 minutes, roll can be unwrapped and sliced or wrapped in plastic wrap and sliced as needed.

Coconut Fruit Balls

1-1/2 cups chopped, dried apricots
2 cups chopped flaked coconut OR desiccated coconut
2/3 cup sweetened condensed milk

Chop apricots and flaked coconut. Blend in sweetened condensed milk. Form candy into small balls. NOTE: Mixture will be drier with desiccated coconut and sweeter with flaked coconut.

Chocolate Butter Mints

2-1/2 cups granulated sugar
1/2 cup brown sugar
2 tablespoons corn syrup
1/8 teaspoon salt
1 cup whole milk
6 tablespoons butter
5 drops peppermint oil
4 drops invertase, optional
4 tablespoons melted semi-sweet chocolate
1/2 cup marshmallow cream
Milk chocolate, melted

In a 3-quart saucepan over medium-high heat combine sugars, corn syrup, salt, milk and butter. Stir frequently as mixture cooks. Curdling may occur but will not affect finished candy. Cook to 239°. Pour on marble slab or other cold surface. Cool to just comfortably warm. Add peppermint oil and invertase. Work candy with fondant paddle. As mixture thickens, add chocolate and marshmallow cream. Blend into mixture. Continue to work candy until it creams and holds shape. Let fondant rest 1 hour. Form into patties. If fondant is too soft, dust hands with flour. Allow patties at least 1 hour to firm up. Dip in milk chocolate.

Peanut Butter Nougat

1 cup invert sugar*, divided
2-1/2 tablespoons dried egg whites
1 cup corn syrup
1/2 cup brown sugar
1/2 teaspoon vanilla
1/4 cup peanut butter
Sweet OR semi-sweet chocolate, melted

*Recipe for invert sugar is on page 52. In a large mixing bowl combine 1/2 cup invert sugar and egg whites. Whip until smooth. Bring corn syrup, brown sugar and remaining invert sugar to a boil. Stir only until boiling starts. Continue cooking without stirring to 230°. Pour hot syrup in thin stream into beating egg white mixture. Mix on low speed to blend. Whip on high speed until light and fluffy. Add vanilla while beating. Cool completely. Add peanut butter to 1 cup of nougat mixture. Stir just to blend. Store remaining nougat mixture in a covered container. Line candy bar molds with melted chocolate. Pat filling into prepared mold. Seal with more chocolate. Chill for 5 minutes. Remove from mold. Makes 8 candy bars.

WHITE CHOCOLATE BASKET WITH MARZIPAN STRAWBERRIES

Molding a Basket:

Plastic mold will be in two halves. Using a brush, line basket with melted white chocolate coating. Let coating set up. Apply another coat. Apply a third coat making sure it is strong enough to stand up. The handle should be filled in solid. Repeat similar process for the other half of basket. When both halves of basket have been completed, place cookie sheet upside down over a burner on the stove. Turn heat on as low as possible. Remove basket halves from molds. Rub each very quickly on hot cookie tray to level edges. Warm each edge enough to adhere to each other. Place halves together quickly and accurately. Let set up. Level bottom of basket by quickly rubbing on hot cookie sheet. Fill the basket with marzipan strawberries. **NOTE:** Candy mold for the basket may be purchased at craft or candy making stores.

Marzipan:
1 cup almond paste
2 egg whites, unbeaten
3 cups confectioners' sugar
1/2 teaspoon vanilla
Red paste food coloring
Course red sugar
Chocolate coating, melted

Knead almond paste until smooth. Add egg whites and mix well. Add sugar, 1 cup at a time. Mix well after each addition. Add vanilla and coloring while kneading. Mold into strawberry shapes by rolling a small piece of marzipan in a ball. Shape one end into a rounded point. Dampen strawberries slightly with brush that has been dipped in water. Roll strawberries in coarse red sugar. Push plastic strawberry stems into wide end of strawberry. Dip bottom half of each strawberry in melted chocolate. Let set up. Arrange strawberries in white chocolate basket.

White Chocolate Basket with Marzipan Strawberries is shown on cover.

Chocolate Candy Molds

The easiest candy to make is made with clear plastic molds and compound chocolate coatings. The molds come in patterns and shapes for nearly every occasion. Special designs can also be created by several of the mold companies.

Compound coatings are available in various forms such as wafer form and by the block. Chocolates also are available in the same forms.

Melting Chocolate

Bring the water to a boil in the bottom of a double boiler. Remove from the stove and place the top of the double boiler containing the coating over hot water. Boiling water under the coating will result in the coating getting too hot. Instead of becoming fluid it will "tighten up", getting so thick it cannot be easily handled.

Melting in a Microwave

Compounds may also be melted very quickly in a microwave. Give them only a minute the first time, stir, then 1/2 minute each time until the compound is nearly melted. Remove from the microwave before all the compound is melted and stir to finish melting.

Flavoring the Candy

Compounds can be flavored with flavoring oils adding variety to molded candies. Remember that liquid causes compound to get thick so only use oils or concentrated flavors which require only a few drops.

Filling the Mold

When the compound is melted, fill the mold cavities using a teaspoon. For an easier, quicker and neater method, fill a squeeze bottle with the melted compound and fill the cavities of the molds.

Use of Squeeze Bottles

Squeeze bottles have proven to be an invaluable aid with the use of chocolate and chocolate compounds. The larger bottles are used to fill bite size molds quickly and neatly. However, they may also be used to fill larger molds or to line molds to make shells that will later be filled.

The smaller size bottle, equipped with a coupler and a small cake decorating tube, is used to apply various colors of coatings to the mold before filling with basic coating color.

Cleaning Squeeze Bottles

The various sizes of squeeze bottles clean very well. Simply pour out all the coating possible and lay the bottles on their sides in the freezer for about 10 minutes. When removed, squeeze the bottle to break up the remaining chocolate left in the bottle and shake it out. It is ready to be melted and used again.

It is best to remove the lid and wash the bottles before putting them back into the freezer. If not, the lid will be hard to remove after it is chilled. This method allows for very little waste of the compound coating.

Keeping Compound Workable

If you are working with a number of molds and wish to keep the coating from setting up in the bottles, turn your oven on the very lowest setting. Place a kitchen towel on a pan and lay the bottles with the chocolate on the towel. The low heat of the oven will keep the chocolate coating from setting up. Now the coating will be ready to use when you need it.

Colorful Candy Molds

Molded candies can be made colorful by first applying appropriate coating colors directly to the mold. Use a small brush or squeeze bottle. Let the colored coating set up and fill the mold cavity with the compound color desired.

Index